SHIRK

According To Scholars From The Four

Madhhabs

Shirk According To Scholars From The Four Madhhabs

1st Edition © Jamiah Media 2011 C.E. / 1432 A.H.

ISBN: 978-0-9567281-1-1

Published by:
Jamiah Media
www.jamiahmedia.com
Email: admin@salafimanhaj.com

Source of translation:
Bayān ush-Shirk wa Wasā'ilihi 'inda 'Ulamā al-Mālikīyyah (Shāriqah: Dār al-Fath, 1415 AH/1994 CE), *Bayān ush-Shirk wa Wasā'ilihi 'inda A'immat al-Hanafiiyyah* (Shāriqah: Dār al-Fath, 1414 AH/1994 CE), *Bayān ush-Shirk wa Wasā'ilihi 'inda 'Ulama al-Shāfi'iyyah* (Shāriqah: Dār al-Fath, 1415 AH/1994 CE) and *Bayān ush-Shirk wa Wasā'ilihi 'inda A'immat al-Hanābilah* (Shāriqah: Dār al-Fath, 1416 AH/1995 CE). Shaykh, Dr Muhammad al-Khumayyis *(hafidhahullāh)* on Monday 7th Muharram 1432 AH/13 December 2010 CE, gave the translator full permission to publish the translation of his series.

Cover design & typesetting:
Ihsaan Design - www.ihsaandesign.co.uk

Edited by Abū Fātimah Azhar Majothī

SHIRK

According To Scholars From The Four

Madhhabs

By Shaykh, Dr. Muhammad al-Khumayyis

(Professor, Faculty of Usul ud-Din, Imam University, Riyadh)

Translated by AbdulHaq Al-Ashanti

◄ Contents ►

⊰ 4. Shirk According To Scholars From The Hanbalī Madhhab ⊱

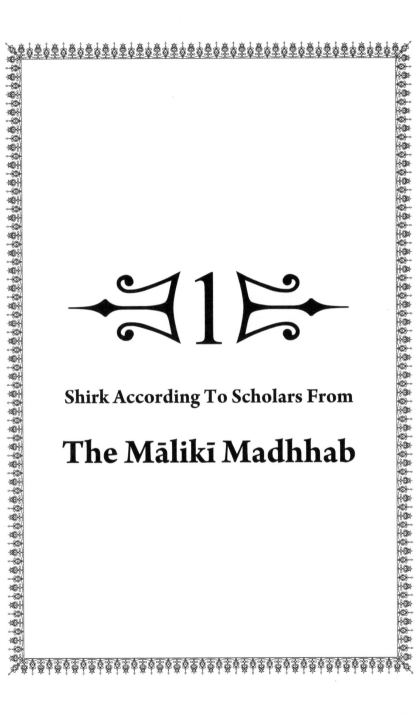

1

Shirk According To Scholars From

The Mālikī Madhhab

⊰ Introduction ⊱

Indeed, all praise is due to Allāh, we praise Him, we seek His aid, and we ask for His forgiveness. We seek refuge in Allāh from the evil of our actions and from the evil consequences of our actions. Whomever Allāh guides, there is none to misguide and whomever Allāh misguides there is none to guide. I bear witness that there is no god worthy of worship except Allāh and I bear witness that Muhammad is the servant and Messenger of Allāh.

﴿يَا أَيُّهَا الَّذِينَ آمَنُواْ اتَّقُواْ اللَّهَ حَقَّ تُقَاتِهِ وَلاَ تَمُوتُنَّ إِلاَّ وَأَنتُم مُّسْلِمُونَ﴾

"O you who have believed, fear Allāh as He should be feared and do not die except as Muslims (in submission to Him)."

{Āli-Imrān (3):102}

﴿يَا أَيُّهَا النَّاسُ اتَّقُواْ رَبَّكُمُ الَّذِي خَلَقَكُم مِّن نَّفْسٍ وَاحِدَةٍ وَخَلَقَ مِنْهَا زَوْجَهَا وَبَثَّ مِنْهُمَا رِجَالاً كَثِيرًا وَنِسَاء وَاتَّقُواْ اللَّهَ الَّذِي تَسَاءلُونَ بِهِ وَالأَرْحَامَ إِنَّ اللَّهَ كَانَ عَلَيْكُمْ رَقِيبًا﴾

"O mankind, fear your Lord, who created you from one soul and created from it its mate and dispersed from both of them

9

many men and women. And fear Allāh through whom you ask things from each other, and (respect) the wombs. Indeed Allāh is ever, over you, an Observer." *{an-Nisā (4):1}*

﴿يَا أَيُّهَا الَّذِينَ آمَنُوا اتَّقُوا اللَّهَ وَقُولُوا قَوْلًا سَدِيدًا يُصْلِحْ لَكُمْ أَعْمَالَكُمْ وَيَغْفِرْ لَكُمْ ذُنُوبَكُمْ وَمَن يُطِعْ اللَّهَ وَرَسُولَهُ فَقَدْ فَازَ فَوْزًا عَظِيمًا﴾

"O you who have believed, fear Allāh and speak words of appropriate justice. He will amend for you your deeds and forgive your sins. And whoever obeys Allāh and His Messenger has certainly attained a great attainment." *{al-Ahzāb (33):70-71}*

The best speech is the Book of Allāh and the best guidance is the guidance of Muhammad ﷺ and the worst of affairs are the newly invented matters for all newly invented matters are an innovation and all innovation is misguidance and all misguidance is in the Fire.

To proceed:

Since the rise of the lights of truth through the sending of the Prophet Muhammad ﷺ and Allāh permitting the perfection of the true *Deen*, the enemies of Allāh, in their various forms, have been grieved: the *yahūd* who were awaiting the Prophet ﷺ disbelieved in him and denied his

Prophethood and thus became hostile towards him; the Persians and Romans viewed his *da'wah* 🌸 as something which will bring an end to their despotic rule and thus they openly declared their enmity against him 🌸; after that, there were the tremendous legions of the Mongols which sacked and pillaged a vast expanse of the Islamic world, and then there were the repeated attacks of the hateful crusaders upon the Islamic lands which are still continuing up until this day in a variety of ways.

All of the above - not to mention others - waged war against the *Deen* of Allāh 🌸, and some of them still do; they have resorted to vile means in this, such as some of them apparently becoming Muslims so as to plot against Islām from within. Those who do this are the worst type and most harmful. Also from them are those who beautify shirk to the Ummah due to the Ummah's ignorance; this is done by dressing shirk in new clothes by way of praising the dead and buried pious (Muslims). This happens currently and is widespread amongst many of those who: attach themselves to *tasawwuf* and worship graves, as is practiced by the ignorant. These practices are present in most Islamic countries, borne out of them changing Allāh's religion into reviving the status of the dead via *shirk* to the extent that it became distant from the *Deen* of Allāh 🌸.[1] They made this appear good to

---

[1] In Northern Nigeria for example, in the western part of the city of Kano, there is a *Qadāriyyah Sufi* burial ground wherein prayers are said to the so-called 'saints' of the *Qadāriyyah Sufi* order. [TN]

the common people via various means such as building domes on graves,[1] decorating them and putting lights on them.[2] They also have custodians who in reality are soothsayers of idolatry who delude the people into making *du'a* to such graves and to seek their needs from them. They also invented weird stories which expressed their assumed abilities and their supernatural powers which as a result, deceived many people. They also wrote books, composed poems and ascribed to them various narrations and all of this was out of their delusion and beautifying *kufr* for them and due to this Allāh ruined them.

Then this disease spread throughout most of the Islamic countries except a few and these few were not saved except by the virtue of Allāh and then the efforts of the righteous full-time scholars and others whom Allāh preserved the *Deen* with and achieved grace with them. Yet the generality of Muslim countries have been eradicated due to this harmful disease to the extent that the affair led to many of them have falling into clear *shirk* which expels one

---

[1] See the '*Zāwiya*' of Hādī bin 'Īsā in the city of Meknes in Morocco: http://members.lycos.nl/hegel/meknes_bestanden/image006.jpg, and the shrine of Mulay Ismā'īl in Fes: http://www.shunya.net/Pictures/Morocco/fes/Fes-Moulay-Idris-shrine.jpg, and http://uweb.txstate.edu/~jh48/zaouia.jpg and in Toubkāl: http://mk23.image.pbase.com/v3/21/512021/4/47447737.MoroccoHoliday2005_08_04I MG_0499.jpg - and all of these take place in a country which claims to be the most vehement in following Imām Mālik ibn Anas 🙵! [TN]

[2] The Barelwīs of the UK during Ramadān utilise Christmas tree lights on their places of worship! [⌐N]

from the religion. They sought their needs from other than Allāh and resorted to other than Allāh for gaining benefit and averting harm and the matter even surpassed this to the extent that some of them began to praise trees and stones and returned to how the people were before during the time of *Jāhiliyyah*. They also intensified travels to tombs and filled their coffers with money, and they indulged in much free-mixing and sought help from the dead in graves by screaming supplications unto them. *There is no power or might except with Allāh, The Most High, The Most Great!*

Then some of those who were associated with Islamic knowledge had these practices of *shirk* beautified to them and were encouraged to do them just as the common people were in the name of knowledge. This reached the extent that those ascribed to knowledge could be divided into three categories:

1. Those who supported such practices of *shirk*, encouraged them, called to them and authored books in order to aid such *shirk* as a *madhhab*, this was all the more the case if they had the material means behind them by which to spread this.

2. Those scholars who knew that such *shirk* was misguidance and was false yet hid the truth out of cowardice, desire or fear, *indeed from Allāh we came and unto Him we shall return.*

3. Those scholars who knew the truth and fought against *shirk* innovations and superstitious beliefs calling the people to pure

13

tawheed and to what the Messenger of Allāh ﷺ, his companions and those who followed, were upon, without fearing the blame of the blamers, hoping only for the Countenance of Allāh. Despite their different schools of thought they are small in number, yet from all of the four *madhāhib* (pl. of *madhhab*) emerged those who supported the *Deen*, warned against *shirk* and called the people to *tawheed*.

So today we are going to present some of the efforts of the Mālikī scholars in this regard and then after we will look at the Shāfi'ī scholars, according to Allāh's facilitation.

The Mālikīs: they attach themselves to the Imām of Madeenah Mālik bin Anas ؓ. He is Mālik bin Anas bin Mālik bin Abī 'Āmir al-Asbahī al-Madanī al-Himyārī, the Imām of Dār ul-Hijrah one of the leaders of the righteous and one of the four famous Imāms. He was born and raised in Madeenah and likewise it was the place of his death. He was at the heart of the *Deen* and he distanced himself from the people in authority and the rulers, holding firm to the truth and not fearing the blame of the blamers. He combined between in-depth *fiqh* and a complete understanding of the *hadeeth* of the Prophet ﷺ; in his *madhhab* he gave importance to the actions of the people of Madeenah as he considered that they held onto what they saw from their fathers and grandfathers - who had accompanied the

Prophet ﷺ, witnessed him and followed him in his *Deen*. He also attached importance to what they were upon in terms of the *Deen*. His *madhhab* spread in many parts of the Islamic world outside of Madeenah, for it spread to Egypt, North Africa, West Africa and Andalusia. The *madhhab* is still the official *madhhab* of many Islamic lands up to today. He died ﷺ in Madeenah in 179 AH after spending most of his life serving the *Deen* in various branches. May Allāh forgive him and bestow on him a great reward.

I ask Allāh to bring benefit with this Book and to make it sincerely for His Countenance and accept it from me sufficient is Allāh for us and He is the Best Guardian, and our final du'ā is all praise is due to Allāh, the Lord of the Worlds.

ᴴ Definition of Shirk According to Some Mālikī Scholars ᴴ

Al-Qāḍī ʿIyyāḍ stated in *Mashāriq ul-Anwār*:

Sheen, rā, kāf: sharikah, with a *fat`ha* on the *sheen* and a *kasrah* on the *rā* is partnership in buying and selling and this is well-known.

Ibn ʾĀshūr stated in explaining the technical meaning of *shirk*:

Associating other than Allāh with Allāh in belief and worship.

Ibn ʾAtiyyah stated:

Those who are made *takfeer* of are all those who worship something with Allāh. Qatādah said that they are the people of *shirk* particularly.

Al-Mīlī al-Mālikī said:

Just as it does not linguistically necessitate ascribing partnership by making the partners have equal shares and portions, it does not just necessitate *shirk* according to the Divine Legislation to equalise a partner for Allāh in all of His Attributes or in one of His Attributes – rather, a person is branded a *Mushrik* in the Divine Legislation due to his affirming associating partners with Allāh - even if he makes the object of association less than Allāh in ability and knowledge for example-; as for what Allāh said about the Mushrikeen,

﴿تَاللَّهِ إِن كُنَّا لَفِي ضَلَالٍ مُّبِينٍ إِذْ نُسَوِّيكُم بِرَبِّ الْعَالَمِينَ﴾

**"By Allāh, we were indeed in manifest error when we equated
you with the Lord of the worlds." *{Shu'arā (26):97-8}***

Their equation here was in regards to obedience and submission not
in regards to ability, like the verse in *Baqarah*,

﴿يُحِبُّونَهُمْ كَحُبِّ اللَّهِ﴾

"They love them as they [should] love Allāh." *{Baqarah (2):165}*

Allāh does not accept that He be associated with Him in worship,
neither with the righteous, nor the sinful, nor the trees, nor stones.
He is not pleased to be associated in worship with those whom He
has favoured from the Prophets, the truthful, the Martyrs and the
pious. Likewise, nothing from the universe is to be associated in
worship with Allāh, neither the sun nor the moon, nor the planets.
The Qur'ān rejects all forms of shirk whatever form it takes, Allāh
says,

﴿إِن كُلُّ مَن فِي السَّمَاوَاتِ وَالْأَرْضِ إِلَّا آتِي الرَّحْمَنِ عَبْدًا﴾

**"There is no one in the heavens and earth but that he comes to
the Most Merciful as a servant." *{Maryam (19):93}***

﴿وَاعْبُدُواْ اللَّهَ وَلاَ تُشْرِكُواْ بِهِ شَيْئًا﴾

"Worship Allāh and do not associate anything in worship with
Him..." *{an-Nisā (4):36}*

﴿وَلاَ يَأْمُرَكُمْ أَن تَتَّخِذُواْ الْمَلاَئِكَةَ وَالنَّبِيِّينَ أَرْبَابًا أَيَأْمُرُكُم بِالْكُفْرِ بَعْدَ إِذْ أَنتُم مُّسْلِمُونَ﴾

"Nor could he order you to take the angels and prophets as lords.
Would he order you to disbelief after you had been Muslims?"
{Āli 'Imrān (3):80}

﴿وَإِذْ قَالَ اللّهُ يَا عِيسَى ابْنَ مَرْيَمَ أَأَنتَ قُلتَ لِلنَّاسِ اتَّخِذُونِي وَأُمِّيَ إِلَـهَيْنِ مِن دُونِ اللّهِ﴾

And [beware the Day] when Allāh will say, "O Jesus, Son of
Mary, did you say to the people, 'Take me and my mother as
deities besides Allāh?'" *{al-Mā'idah (5):116}*

This is our exposition of *shirk* according to the Divine Legislation, if
it was lengthy then we intended by that to simplify it for the general
people and silence the stubborn.[1]

Imām Mālik defined *at-Ṭāghūt* as being:

All that is worshipped other than Allāh.[1]

---

[1] *Risālat ush-Shirk*, pp.64-5

The *tāghūt* is all that transgresses the limits and we know that Islām is not affirmed for a person until he or she primarily disbelieves in *tāghūt:*

﴿فَمَنْ يَكْفُرْ بِالطَّاغُوتِ وَيُؤْمِنْ بِاللّهِ فَقَدِ اسْتَمْسَكَ بِالْعُرْوَةِ الْوُثْقَىٰ﴾

"So whoever disbelieves in tāghūt and believes in Allāh has grasped the most trustworthy handhold with no break in it."
{Baqarah (2):256}

﴿وَلَقَدْ بَعَثْنَا فِي كُلِّ أُمَّةٍ رَّسُولاً أَنِ اعْبُدُواْ اللّهَ وَاجْتَنِبُواْ الطَّاغُوتَ﴾

And We certainly sent into every nation a Messenger, [saying], "Worship Allāh and avoid tāghūt." *{an-Nahl (16):36}*

So a Muslim firstly has to disbelieve in the *tāghūt* that are worshipped other than Allāh or that are obeyed in disobedience to Allāh, or referred to for judgement other than the rule of Allāh, or that are glorified other than Allāh. So disbelieving in *tāghūt* has to be ascertained before *īmān* in Allāh; *īmān* in Allāh and in the *tāghūt* cannot be present in a person.

Indeed, these very *tawāghīt* (pl. of *tāghūt*) on the Day of Judgement will free themselves from the worship which was directed to them by those who worshipped them other than Allāh, as Allāh says,

﴿إِذْ تَبَرَّأَ الَّذِينَ اتُّبِعُواْ مِنَ الَّذِينَ اتَّبَعُواْ وَرَأَوُاْ الْعَذَابَ وَتَقَطَّعَتْ بِهِمُ الأَسْبَابُ﴾

---

[1] *Fath ul-Majeed*, p.566

"[And they should consider that] when those who have been followed disassociate themselves from those who followed [them], and they [all] see the punishment, and cut off from them are the ties [of relationship]..." *{Baqarah (2):166}*

﴿إِنَّا بُرَءَاء مِنكُمْ وَمِمَّا تَعْبُدُونَ مِن دُونِ اللَّهِ كَفَرْنَا بِكُمْ وَبَدَا بَيْنَنَا وَبَيْنَكُمُ الْعَدَاوَةُ وَالْبَغْضَاء أَبَدًا حَتَّى تُؤْمِنُوا بِاللَّهِ وَحْدَهُ﴾

"Indeed, we are disassociated from you and from whatever you worship other than Allāh. We have denied you, and there has appeared between us and you animosity and hatred forever until you believe in Allāh alone." *{al-Mumtahinah (60):4}*

Within the statements of Imām Mālik ﷺ, it is clear that the *tāghūt* according to him includes all that is worshipped other than Allāh. So desires are a *tāghūt*; Shaytān is a *tāghūt*; a tree that is worshipped is a *tāghūt*; a stone that is worshipped is a *tāghūt*; a leader who substitutes (the Divine Legislation of Allāh) is a *tāghūt*; whoever commands the people to obey him via disobeying Allāh is a *tāghūt* and likewise all that which is worshipped other than Allāh. However within some narrations Mālik restricted the last one (i.e. whoever commands the people to obey him via disobeying Allāh is a *tāghūt*) to apply to those who were pleased with this worship so as not to include those who are worshipped without their being pleased with this, such as the Messiah, his mother, 'Uzayr and others, peace be upon them.

⇥ The Categories of Shirk According to the Mālikī Scholars ⇤

Shirk intrinsically opposes *tawheed* as has proceeded, so it is obligatory for the Muslim to know what *shirk* is and its categories: major, minor, apparent and hidden – so as to avoid them all and protect his/her *Deen*; this will not be accomplished except by knowing these types and being warned from them in order to block the means to them.

Imām al-Hāfidh Ibn al-'Arabī al-Mālikī stated:

> Shirk has categories, the main two being: related to beliefs; related to actions. If shirk is in beliefs then there is no salvation or redemption from this and if shirk is in regards to actions then it is hoped that there could be salvation (for the one who committed the action).[1]

Al-Mīlī al-Mālikī said:

> The categories of *shirk* are mentioned in the verse from *Sūrah Sabā'*,

$$﴿قُلِ ادْعُوا الَّذِينَ زَعَمْتُم مِّن دُونِ اللَّهِ لَا يَمْلِكُونَ مِثْقَالَ ذَرَّةٍ فِي السَّمَاوَاتِ وَلَا فِي$$

$$الْأَرْضِ وَمَا لَهُمْ فِيهِمَا مِن شِرْكٍ وَمَا لَهُ مِنْهُم مِّن ظَهِيرٍ$$

---

[1] *'Āridah al-Ahwadhī* (Beirut: Dār ul-Kutub al-'Ilmiyyah, n.d.), vol.10, p.106.

$$\text{وَلَا تَنفَعُ الشَّفَاعَةُ عِندَهُ إِلَّا لِمَنْ أَذِنَ لَهُ}$$

"Say, [O Muhammad], "Invoke those you claim [as deities] besides Allāh." They do not possess an atom's weight [of ability] in the heavens or on the earth, and they do not have therein any partnership [with Him], nor is there for Him from among them any assistant. And intercession does not benefit with Him except for one whom He permits." *{Saba' (34):22-23}*

The verse includes four categories of *shirk* which are:

Firstly: shirk of possession, Allāh negates that other than Him can possess anything independent of Him, even if it is as insignificant as a mustard seed.

Secondly: shirk of ownership, Allāh negates that other than Him has a portion in His dominion, regardless of how this portion is in place and status.

Thirdly: shirk in assistance, Allāh negates that He has an assistant or helper who assists anything with Him in the same way as one of us would need a helper to carry provisions for example.

Fourthly: *shirk* in intercession, Allāh negates that there exists one who can present himself to Him with his status in order to save others via his intercession. So Allāh does not accept any of the types of association, even the lightest and most hidden of them which is shirk by status in order to gain salvation and success - except, after permission of the Intercessor (and) intercession is only for Allāh.

After this explanation, we bring attention to the fact that the Shaykh ﷻ did not cover *shirk* in *Ulūhiyyah* and *Tawheed ul-Ulūhiyyah* which is the foundation of the *Deen* of Islām and over which the Messengers argued with their people. *Tawheed ul-Ulūhiyyah* was what all of the Prophets came with, as Allāh says,

﴿وَمَا أَرْسَلْنَا مِن قَبْلِكَ مِن رَّسُولٍ إِلَّا نُوحِي إِلَيْهِ أَنَّهُ لَا إِلَهَ إِلَّا أَنَا فَاعْبُدُونِ﴾

"And We sent not before you any messenger except that We revealed to him that, There is no deity except Me, so worship Me." *{al-Anbiyā (21):25}*

So this is inability from him ﷺ #, wherein he gives importance to explaining *shirk* in *Rubūbiyyah* yet neglects any referral to *shirk* in *Ulūhiyyah* and *'Ibādah*, even though to focus on *Ulūhiyyah* takes precedence as it is what has engulfed the *Ummah* and not *shirk* in *Rubūbiyyah*.

⊰ Preventing the Means That Lead to Shirk According to the Mālikī Scholars ⊱

Before we start to explain the means to *shirk* according to the Mālikī scholars, we will clarify the meaning of the means (*dharā'i*) as is found within their books.

Ash-Shātibī said:

> The reality of the means is to seek nearness with what is beneficial to that which is harmful.[1]

Al-Qurtubī said:

> The means are an expression of what is not prohibited in itself but it is feared that whoever takes such means will fall into that which is prohibited.[2]

It has been transmitted from Imām Mālik and some of his followers that they prohibited all means to *shirk* such as: plastering over graves (in order to

---

[1] *Al-Muwāfiqāt*, vol.4, p.198
[2] *Tafseer ul-Qurtubī*, vol.2, p.58

make them permanent structures),[1] writing on them,[2] building on them,[3] taking them as *masājid*,[4] facing them in *du'ā'*,[1] prostrating to them,[2] praying

---

[1] It is reported in Muslim from Jābir ﷺ who said: *"The Messenger of Allah ﷺ forbade that the graves should be plastered (made into permanent structures), used as sitting places (for the people) or building over them."* To know more about the position of Mālik and his followers with regards to this issue refer to: *al-Mudawwana*, vol.1, p.189; Ibn 'AbdulBarr, *Kitāb ul-Kāfī*, vol.1, p.283; *Tanweer ul-Maqālah*, vol.3, p.40; *Thamr ud-Dānee*, p.230; and *Tafseer ul-Qurtubī*, vol.10, p.380.

[2] Based on what was reported by Abū Dāwūd, at-Tirmidhī and others from the *hadeeth* of Jābir ﷺ that the Messenger of Allāh ﷺ *"forbade that the graves should be plastered (made into permanent structures) and that they be written on."* To know more about the position of Imām Mālik and of many of his followers in regards to this issue refer to *Fath ul-Majeed*, p.323.

[3] Based upon what Muslim reported from Jābir ﷺ that *"The Messenger of Allah ﷺ forbade that the graves should be plastered (made into permanent structures), used as sitting places (for the people) or building over them."* To know more about the position of Mālik and his followers with regards to this issue refer to: *al-Mudawwana*, vol.1, p.189; *al-Mi'ār ul-Mu'rab*, vol.1, p.317-18; *Tanweer ul-Maqālah*, vol.3, p.39; *Thamr ud-Dānī*, p.231; and *Tafseer ul-Qurtubī*, vol.10, p.379; *Fath ul-Majeed*, p.323; *Tayseer ul-'Azeez al-Hamd*, p.323-24 and Ibn 'AbdulBarr, *al-Kāfī*, vol.1, p.283.

[4] The Prophet ﷺ said: *"Allāh cursed the yāhūd and the nasārā because they took the graves of their prophets as Masājid."* The hadeeth is agreed upon. He ﷺ also said ﷺ: *"Those before you used to take the graves of their Prophets as Masājid, do not take graves as Masājid! I forbid you from doing that!"* Reported by Muslim and others. In order to know more about the position of the Mālikī scholars in this regard refer to: *at-Tamheed*, vol.1, p.168, vol.5, p.45; *al-Muntaqā*, vol.7, p.195; *Tafseer ul-Qurtubī*, vol.10, p.380; az-Zurqānī, *Sharh ul-Muwatta' Mālik*, vol.4, p.233, vol.12, p.351; *Tayseer ul-'Azeez al-Hameed*, p.240; *al-Muntaqā*, vol.1, pp.306-07.

on them,[3] travelling to them, for travel should only be to the three *masājid*.[4]

Al-Qurtubī said:

Taking a firm hold of the preventative means is the madhhab of Mālik and his companions, it is also the madhhab of Ahmad bin Hanbal according to a narration from him. The Book and the Sunnah also indicate this basis.[5]

He (Al-Qurtubī) also said:

For this reason it reached the Muslims that they should prevent the means (to shirk) in regards to the grave of the Prophet ﷺ. They raised the walls to encompass it and blocked off the entrance to it as

---

[1] Muslim and others reported that the Prophet ﷺ said: *"Do not sit on graves and to not pray on them."* To know more about the position of Mālik and his followers with regards to this issue refer to: *Siyānat ul-Insān*, p.264; *Fath ul-Mannān*, pp.358-59 and *Tayseer ul-'Azeez al-Hameed*, p.358.

[2] In order to know more about the position of the Mālikī scholars in this regard refer to: *at-Tamheed*, vol.6, p.383, vol.1, p.167 and vol.5, p.45.

[3] It has been reported by Muslim and others that the Prophet ﷺ said, *"Do not sit on graves and to not pray on them."* In order to know more about the position of the Mālikī scholars in this regard refer to: *Muqaddimat Ibn Rushd*, p.174; *at-Tamheed*, vol.1, p.167, vol.5, p.25 and vol.6, p.283; *Tafseer ul-Qurtubī*, vol.10, p.379.

[4] Based on the saying of the Prophet ﷺ, *"Do not travel except to the three Masājid..."* In order to know more about the position of the Mālikī scholars in this regard refer to: *al-Mu'allim*, vol.12, p.82; az-Zurqānī, *Sharh Mukhtasar Khaleel*, vol.3, p.93; *Tayseer ul-'Azeez al-Hameed*, p.361; az-Zurqānī, *Sharh ul-Muwatta'*, vol.1, pp224-25.

[5] *Tafseer ul-Qurtubī*, vol.12, pp.57-8.

they feared that his grave would be taken as a Qiblah for people to face it in their prayer as an act of worship. They built two walls at the corners of the grave and diverted them in order to form a triangular angle to the north so that it would not be possible for anyone to face his grave.[1]

Imām Mālik said:

Plastering graves is detested and so is building on them, these are stones which have been built on.[2]

Ibn Abī Shāmah stated:

Mālik and other 'Ulama from Madeenah disliked going to those masājid and relics in Madeenah including even if it was just a dome.[3]

Ibn 'AbdulBāqī stated in his explanation of *al-Muwatta'*:

Ashhab reported from Mālik that he disliked burial within a masjid and said: So if he prevented this then the rest of the Prophet's relics are more deserving than this and Mālik also disliked seeking pleasure by visiting the location of the tree where the allegiance was pledged

---

[1] *Qurrat ul-'Uyyūn*, p.136

[2] *Al-Mudawwana*, vol.1, p.189

[3] *Al-Bā'ith 'alā Inkār al-Bida' wa'l-Hawādith*, pp.96-97; *Kitāb Ibn Wadāh*, no.113

to the Prophet (ﷺ), in order to differ from the yahood and the nasāra.[1]

Al-Qurtubī said:

Our scholars have said that it is prohibited for the Muslims to take the graves of the Prophets and of the *'Ulama* as *masājid*.[2]

Ibn Rushd stated:

If the Janāzah prayer has ended it should not continue to be a means for prayer on graves and this is the *madhhab* of Ashhab and Sahnūn.[3]

Ibn Rushd also said:

Mālik hated building on graves and adorning graves with paving stones and tiles.[4]

Al-Qurtubī said in explaining the *hadeeth* of the Prophet ﷺ, *"Do not pray on graves and do not sit on them"*:

Meaning: do not take them as a *Qiblah* to pray on or towards like the *Yāhūd* and the *Nasārā* do, as this leads to worship of the one who is in the grave which was a reason for idol-worship. The Prophet ﷺ

---

[1] *Tayseer ul-'Azeez al-Hameed*, p.340.

[2] *Tafseer ul-Qurtubī*, vol.10, p.380

[3] *Muqaddimah Ibn Rushd*, p.174

[4] *Fath ul-Majeed*, p.323 – it may be the case that he intends what is called today engravings on graves wherein the name of the deceased, along with the date of death, is written and Allāh knows best.

warned against doing the like of this and prevented the means that lead to that idol-worship.[1]

Then al-Qurtubī said:

As for building constructions (on graves) in a way similar to that of Jāhiliyyah out of pride and veneration then that has been destroyed and has disappeared, for within that was adorning the first port of call of the Herefafter (i.e. the grave) with things from the dunya resembling those who has venerated graves and worshipped them.[2]

Imām Mālik said:

I do not view that one should stand by the grave of the Prophet ﷺ and make *du'ā*, rather one should give *salām* and then pass by.

This was mentioned by Ismā'īl bin Ishāq in *al-Mabsūt* and its *isnad* is *Saheeh* as noted in *Siyānat ul-Insān*.[3]

He also said in *al-Mabsūt*:

There is no harm in one who has arrived from a journey or has departed on one to stand by the grave of the Prophet ﷺ and make *du'ā* for him, Abū Bakr and 'Umar.

It was said to him:

---

[1] *Tafseer ul-Qurtubī*, vol.10, p.380

[2] Ibid., vol.10, p.381

[3] *Siyānat ul-Insān*, p.264; *Fath ul-Mannān*, p.358

Some people from Madeenah do not arrive from a journey or depart on one except that they do that once or more and they may even stand by the grave on Jumua'ah or on other days of the week at any one time or more than once, sending salutations and making du'ā for an hour or so.

Then he said:

These actions have not reached me from any of the people of fiqh in our land, so to leave these practices is better. The latter part of this Ummah will not be rectified except with that which rectified the first part of the Ummāh. It has not reached me from the former part of the Ummah that they did that...[1]

As for the story that has been mentioned by Qādī 'Iyyād from Muhammad bin Humayd who said:

Abu Ja'far al-Mansūr, the leader of the believers, discussed with Imām Mālik in the Masjid of the Messenger of Allāh ﷺ and Mālik said to him: O leader of the believers do not raise your voice in this masjid for Allāh has said,

$$﴿لَا تَرْفَعُوا أَصْوَاتَكُمْ فَوْقَ صَوْتِ النَّبِيِّ﴾$$

---

[1] *Fath il-Mannān*, p.358

"...do not raise your voices above the voice of the Prophet..."

{al-Hujurāt (49): 2}

Then Qādī 'Iyyād said:

This story as it has been documented in this way is either weak or distorted.[1]

As for the story which has been reported by Qādī 'Iyyād with an *isnad* from Mālik in the story of his dialogue with Abū Mansūr and that Mālik said: O Abū Abdullāh (Imām Mālik), should I face the *Qiblah* and make *dua'* or face the Messenger of Allāh and make *duā*?

Abū Abdullāh (Imām Mālik) said:

Do not avert your face from him (i.e. the messenger of Allāh ﷺ) for he is your means, and likewise the means of your father Adam, to Allāh until the Day of Resurrection. So rather you should face him (i.e. the Messenger of Allāh) and seek intercession via him so that he will intercede for you with Allāh.[2]

The author of *Tayseer ul-'Azeez al-Hameed* stated:

---

[1] *Siyānat ul-Insān*, p.255; *Fath ul-Mannān*, p.359

[2] *Tayseer ul-'Azeez al-Hameed*, p.358

This narration is either weak or fabricated because in its chain of transmission is Muhammad bin Hameed who has been impugned (i.e. criticised).[1]

As for what was narrated by Ibn Zibālah regarding the reports of Madeenah from 'Umar bin Hārūn from Salamah bin Wardān (and they are both *sāqit* [weak and thus to be dropped])[2] that he said: I saw Anas bin Mālik give salutations to the Prophet ﷺ, then he turned his back to the grave and made *duā*. The two men are *sāqit* as found in *Tayseer ul-'Azeez al-Hameed*.

As for the story wherein Mālik recited the following verse,

﴿وَلَوْ أَنَّهُمْ إِذ ظَّلَمُواْ أَنفُسَهُمْ جَآؤُوكَ فَاسْتَغْفَرُواْ اللَّهَ وَاسْتَغْفَرَ لَهُمُ الرَّسُولُ﴾

"And if, when they wronged themselves, they had come to you, [O Muhammad], and asked forgiveness of Allāh and the Messenger had asked forgiveness for them..." {an-Nisā (4): 64}

Then the story is *bātil* and Allāh knows best. It has not been mentioned by anyone from the Ummah from what I know and none has mentioned that Mālik recommended that one can be asked of anything or sought

---

[1] Ibid.

[2] [TN]: Al-Hāfidh Ibn Hajar stated in *at-Taqreeb* about 'Umar bin Hārūn: **"matrook, but he was a hāfidh"**.

forgiveness after death. His documented statements negate this as stated by the author of *Fath ul-Mannān*.[1]

Al-Qurtubī said:

> And as for the Sunnah then there are many affirmed authentic *ahādeeth*, such as the hadeeth of Ā'ishah ؊ wherein Umm Habībah and Umm Salamah ؊ mentioned the church that they had seen in Ethiopia wherein pictures were displayed. They mentioned this to the Messenger of Allāh ﷺ and he said: "*They were the ones that if a righteous man among them died they would make his grave into a masjid and make images of the person within it. They are the worst of creation with Allāh.*" Reported by Bukhari and Muslim.[2]
>
> Our scholars have said: they early generations done that in order to see their images and be reminded of their piety so as to strive as their pious people did and worship Allāh at their graves. Yet as time passed the generations after them became ignorant of the purpose of these images and then Shaytān whispered into them that their fathers and grandparents used to actually worship these images – so then the people began to worship the images. The Prophet ﷺ cautioned

---

[1] *Fath ul-Mannān*, p.360

[2] Reported by Bukhārī, vol.3, p.247, *hadeeth* no.1341 in *Janā'iz*, '*Chapter on Building a Masjid over a Grave*'; Muslim, vol.1, p.375, *hadeeth* no.528 in *al-Masājid wa Mawādi' us-Salah*, '*Chapter on the Prohibition of Building Masājid over Graves*' – the *hadeeth* is via Hishām bin 'Urwah from his father from Ā'ishah ؊.

against this and gave a stern warning against doing the likes of such things.[1]

Ibn ul-Hajj said in *al-Madkhal*:

It is not permissible to make *tawāf* around tombs as *tawāf* is only to be made around the Ancient House (i.e. the Ka'ba). Likewise, it is not legislated to kiss or give salutations to any place except the Ancient House and likewise it is not legislated to kiss or give salutations to anything except the Black Stone.[2]

At-Tartūshī said:

Muhammad bin Wadāh narrated that 'Umar bin al-Khattāb ﷺ instructed that the tree under which the Prophet was pledged allegiance to, be chopped down as the people would go to it and 'Umar feared that it would cause a *fitna* to the people. Mālik and other 'Ulama from Madeenah disliked going to those *masājid* and relics which were in Madeenah even if it was one dome.[3]

At-Tartūshī also said:

'Umar ibn al-Khattāb said that: those before you were destroyed because they used to worship the relics of their Prophets and take them as churches and monasteries. Whoever has to pray and passes

---

[1] *Tafseer ul-Qurtubī*, vol.2, p.58

[2] Ibn ul-Hajj, *al-Madkhal* – as is noted in *al-Mushāhadāt ul-Ma'sūmiyyah*, p.73

[3] *Kitāb ul-Hawādith wa'l-Bida*, pp.294-95

by one of these places should pray in them but whoever does not have to pray, should not pray within them.[1]

---

[1] Ibid., pp.308-09

❧ Samples of Shirk Which the Mālikī Scholars Have Cautioned Against ☙

It has been documented from Imām Mālik and from some of his followers that there is a prohibition against various types of major and minor *shirk*, *du'ā* to other than Allāh,[1] seeking help from other than Allāh,[2] making vows to other than Allāh,[3] slaughtering for other than Allāh,[1] believing that the

---

[1] Based on Allāh's saying, **"And your Lord says, "Call upon Me; I will respond to you." Indeed, those who disdain My worship will enter Hell [rendered] contemptible."** *{Ghāfir (40): 60}* And Allāh's saying, **"And who is more astray than he who invokes besides Allāh those who will not respond to him until the Day of Resurrection? And they, of their invocation, are unaware."** *{al-Ahqāf (46): 5}.* And also based on the saying of the Prophet ﷺ : *"Du'ā is worship."* For more on this topic from the Mālikī scholars refer to al-Mīlī, *Risālat ush-Shirk,* p.192 and *Tahreer wa't-Tanweer,* vol.24, p.181 and vol.26, p.11

[2] Allāh says, **[Remember] when you asked help of your Lord, and He answered you, "Indeed, I will reinforce you with a thousand from the angels, following one another."** *{al-Anfāl (8): 9}* And Allāh says,**"...while they call to Allāh for help..."** *{al-Ahqāf (46): 17}* See *Tahreer wa't-Tanweer,* vol.9, pp.274-75, vol.26, p.39

[3] Allāh says, **"Then let them end their untidiness and fulfil their vows and perform tawāf around the ancient House."** *{al-Hajj (22): 29}* Vows are worship which have to be for Allāh, see *Tahreer wa't-Tanweer,* vol.17, p.248; *Tayseer ul-'Azeez al-Hameed,* p.207 and al-Mīlī, *Risālat ush-Shirk,* p.268. It is not permissible to make a vow to a Walī, a Prophet or anyone else as this is shirk because worship would be directed to other than Allāh. Many of the ignorant people make vows at the graves of al-Badawī, al-Husayn, al-Jīlānī or others. All of this is clear association of partners in worship with Allāh and there is no

Awliyā have an influence in the universe along with Allāh,[2] believing that someone along with Allāh knows the unseen,[3] swearing oaths to other than Allāh[4] or believing that the stars have an effect in bringing down the rain

---

room whatsoever to claim that **"The vow is for Allāh and the reward is for the Walī"** as is stated by some ignoramuses, this is void and it not accepted by clear intelligence.

[1] Based on Allāh's saying, **"So pray to your Lord and sacrifice [to Him alone]."** *{al-Kawthar (108): 2}* And Allāh's saying, Say, **"Indeed, my prayer, my rites of sacrifice, my living and my dying are for Allāh, Lord of the worlds."** *{al-An'ām (6): 162}* Slaughtering is an act of worship which has to be only for Allāh, in the name of Allāh, it is not permissible to eat that which has been slaughtered without the name of Allāh being mentioned on it. See *Mukhtasar Khaleel*, vol.3, p.130; *Tafseer ul-Qurtubī*, vol.2, p.224 and *Tahreer wa't-Tanweer*, vol.30, p.574.

[2] This is *shirk* in *Rubūbiyyah* and Allāh negates that anything else can have an influence within the universe apart from Him, **Say, [O Muhammad], "Invoke those you claim [as deities] besides Allāh." They do not possess an atom's weight [of ability] in the heavens or on the earth, and they do not have therein any partnership [with Him], nor is there for Him from among them any assistant. And intercession does not benefit with Him except for one whom He permits."** *{Saba' (34): 22-23}* This issue in light of the verse has been discussed prior in detail. Refer to az-Zurqānī, *Sharh ul-Muwatta'*, vol.1, p.347; al-Bājī, *Sharh ul-Muwatta'*, vol.1, p.334 and *Tahreer wa't-Tanweer*, vol.22, pp.185-191.

[3] Based on Allāh's saying, **"[He is] Knower of the unseen, and He does not disclose His [knowledge of the] unseen to anyone..."** *{Jinn (72): 26}* Allāh also says, **"Say, "None in the heavens and earth knows the unseen except Allāh,"...** *{an-Naml (27): 65}* Refer to: Ibn al-'Arabī, *Ahkām ul-Qur'ān*, vol.2, pp.738-39; *Tafseer ul-Qurtubī*, vol.1, p.290 and al-Mīlī, *Risālat ush-Shirk*, p.137.

[4] Based on what the Prophet ﷺ said: *"Whoever swears by other than Allāh has committed shirk."* And in another wording *"...has committed kufr."* See *at-Tamheed*, vol.14, pp.366-67; *Tafseer ul-Qurtubī*, vol.10, p.40, vol.6, p.270-71; ad-Dārdīrī, *Sharh as-Sagheer*, vol.2, p.203; Ibn Rushd, *al-Muqadimmāt*, pp.308-09; *Sharh Rizq 'alā matn ar-Risālat*, vol.2,

(and having other effects in the universe)[1] and having trust in other than Allāh.[2]

Ibn al-'Arabī stated:

The stations of the unseen are five which only Allāh knows about and that He informed the truthful one about (i.e. the Prophet) regarding the signs of the Hour. Whoever claims that it will definitely rain tomorrow is a disbeliever and so is the one who claims to know what is in the wombs. As for the one who claims to know the future then he is a disbeliever and as for the one who claims to know what will happen in the universe before it has actually happened is also a disbeliever without doubt. As for the one who informs about an eclipse of the sun and the moon then our scholars have said about such a person that: he is to be punished and imprisoned, he is not to be made *takfeer* of and the absence of making *takfeer* is based on what a group of scholars have said that it is something which can be calculated and this in itself is something which Allāh informs about when He says,

---

p.15; *al-Mu'allim*, vol.2, p.240; *Sharh az-Zurqānī 'alā Mukhtasar Khaleel*, vol.3, p.53 and *Kitāb ul-Kāfī fī Fiqh Ahl ul-MaDeenah al-Mālikī*, vol.1, p.448.

[1] *Al-Muntaqā Sharh ul-Muwatta' Mālik*, vol.1, p.334 and *Sharh az-Zurqānī 'alā Mukhtasar Khaleel*.

[2] Based on Allāh's saying, "**...and upon their Lord they rely...**" *{al-Anfāl (8): 2}* See Ibn 'Āshūr, *at-Tahreer wa't-Tanweer*, vol.9, p.259.

41

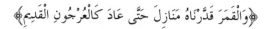

"And the moon We have determined for it phases, until it returns [appearing] like the old date stalk." *{Yāseen (36): 39}*

So due to the fact that it can be calculated our scholars refrained from making *takfeer* of those people who claim to be able to determine its movement. As for their punishment that is on account of the doubt they cause to the general public which is connected to knowledge of the Unseen and a person not knowing the difference between the two. Also the person is punished for confusing the people's understanding of the *Deen* and destabilising its principles in regards to certainty. As a result, they are punished until they are to keep to themselves if they are well-known and they are not to publicise their actions.[1]

Ibn 'AbdulBarr stated:

It is not permissible to swear an oath to other than Allāh ﷻ for anything at all in any circumstances whatsoever. There is consensus on this and it has been reported from Sa'eed bin 'Ubaydah from Ibn 'Umar that he heard the Messenger of Allāh ﷺ say: *"Whoever swears an oath to other than Allāh has committed shirk."* Mentioned by Abū

---

[1] *Ahkām ul-Qur'ān*, vol.2, pp.738-39

Dāwūd[1] and others. Muhammad ibn Sīrīn reported from Abu Hurayrah who said: The Messenger of Allāh ﷺ said: *"Do not swear oaths by your fathers, by your mothers or by deities other than Allāh, only swear by Allāh and do not swear by Allāh except if you are truthful."*[2].......[3]

Ibn Rushd stated:

What is cautioned against is to swear an oath by al-Lāt, al-'Uzza, *tawāgheet* and by anything that is worshipped other than Allāh. This is because swearing oaths by something is glorifying it and glorifying these things is *kufr* in Allāh.[4]

Al-Qurtubī stated within his *tafseer* of the saying of Allāh,

$$﴿وَمَا أُهِلَّ بِهِ لِغَيْرِ اللَّهِ﴾$$

---

[1] Ahmad, vol.1, pp.34-125; at-Tirmidhī, vol.4, p.110, *hadeeth* no.1535 in *Nudhūr ul-Īmān*; Abū Dāwūd, vol.3, p.278, *hadeeth* no.3251 in *Kitāb ul-Īmān* and the chapter of the dislike of swearing oaths by fathers; Ibn Hibbān, vol.6, p.278, *hadeeth* no.4343; al-Hākim, vol.4, p.297, al-Hākim said that the *hadeeth* is Saheeh according to the conditions of Shaykhayn and adh-Dhahabī agreed with him. Tirmidhī said that the hadeeth is *hasan* via the route of Sa'd bin 'Ubaydah from Ibn 'Umar in *marfū'* form, al-Albānī authenticated in *Saheeh ul-Jāmi' as-Sagheer*, vol.2, p.1168, *hadeeth* no.6204.

[2] Reported by Abū Dāwūd vol.3, p.569, *hadeeth* 3248 in *Kitāb ul-Īmān* and the chapter of the dislike of swearing oaths by fathers – form the narration of Muhammad bin Sīreen from Abū Hurayrah in *marfū'* form.

[3] Ibn 'AbdulBarr, *at-Tamheed*, vol.14, pp.366-67

[4] *Muqaddamāt Ibn Rushd*, p.309

"...and that which has been dedicated to other than Allāh."

{Baqarah (2): 173}

Meaning: the name of other than Allāh was mentioned on it such as the food that has been slaughtered by the Mājūs, the idolator and the Mu'attil, for the idolator slaughters for the idol, the Mājūsī slaughters for the fire and the Mu'attil does without with a belief in anything rather he slaughters for himself. There is no difference of opinion among the scholars that whatever the Mājūsī slaughters for his fire and whatever the idolator slaughters for his idol – is not to be eaten.[1]

Al-Mīlī stated:

Calling upon other than Allāh is clear shirk and filthy kufr, there are two types to it: one of them is to call upon other than Allāh with Allāh, for example "O my Lord, O my Shaykh", "O my Lord and my Grandfather", "O Allāh and His people", "O Allāh and my master 'AbdulQādir" and I have heard many people say the likes of this and people have heard some other people say "O my Lord (Yā Rabbi) and O my master Yūsuf, forgive me" and the Yusuf they intend here is one of the children of the righteous (in Algeria). The shirk within these calls is clear because the caller associates Allāh in

---

[1] *Tafseer ul Qurtubī*, vol.2, pp.223-224

his call my adding a *waw* (lit. 'and') or by not using it. It indicates the association in worship and the thing being associated is included within the *duā* of worship. The second type: Calling upon other than Allāh such as the one who calls upon a man or upon the dead pious........[1]

Ibn 'AbdulBarr said:

It is prohibited for the Muslims to take the graves of the Prophets, *'Ulama* and Righteous as *masājid*.[2]

He also said:

An idol is an image made from gold, silver or any other material for a statue and includes all that which is worshipped other than Allāh, whether this is a carved idol or not. The Arabs used to pray to idols and worship them, the Messenger of Allāh ﷺ feared that his Ummah would do what was done by the nations before that: when a Prophet died they would gather around his grave as is done with idols. As a result, he said ﷺ: *"O Allāh do not make my grave an idol that is worshipped."* Meaning to pray and prostrate to it and worship it, Allāh's Anger is severe on the one who does this and the Messenger of Allāh ﷺ used to caution his companions from it. The Messenger of Allāh ﷺ informed of the destruction and wrath that we befall the

---

[1] *Risālat ush-Shirk*, p.192

[2] Ibn 'AbdulBarr, *at-Tamheed*, vol.1, p.168

people from Allāh if they commit this major *shirk* which does not please Allāh, as he ﷺ feared that what happened to the people befall would befall the Ummah also.[1]

Al-Mīlī stated:

The similarity of this Ummah with those before them is in terms of the Divine *Sunan*: what befall the Arabs and those before them will befall others after them if they are ignorant of the principles of the *Deen* and went to excess in seeking blessings from the dead pious, Allāh says,

﴿سُنَّةَ اللَّهِ الَّتِى قَدْ خَلَتْ مِن قَبْلُ وَلَن تَجِدَ لِسُنَّةِ اللَّهِ تَبْدِيلاً﴾

"[This is] the established way of Allāh which has occurred before. And never will you find in the way of Allāh any change."

{al-Fath (48): 23}

The scholars have consensus on saying "history repeats itself".

<u>Samples of Comtemporary Idolatry:</u>

If it is said to the people that those tombs and shrines are idols they would say "you are insulting the pious!" O my brothers understand the Arabic language well and also the *Deen* and then you will find that it is not insulting the *Awliyā*. For anything that is ascribed for

---

[1] Ibid., vol.5, p.45

worship other than Allāh is an idol and all who worship it are destroyed, but not all that is worshipped is destroyed, Allāh says,

﴿ إِنَّكُمْ وَمَا تَعْبُدُونَ مِن دُونِ ٱللَّهِ حَصَبُ جَهَنَّمَ أَنتُمْ لَهَا وَٰرِدُونَ. لَوۡ كَانَ هَٰٓؤُلَآءِ ءَالِهَةً مَّا وَرَدُوهَا ۖ وَكُلٌّ فِيهَا خَٰلِدُونَ. لَهُمۡ فِيهَا زَفِيرٌ وَهُمۡ فِيهَا لَا يَسۡمَعُونَ. إِنَّ ٱلَّذِينَ سَبَقَتۡ لَهُم مِّنَّا ٱلۡحُسۡنَىٰٓ أُوْلَٰٓئِكَ عَنۡهَا مُبۡعَدُونَ ﴾

"Indeed, you [disbelievers] and what you worship other than Allāh are the firewood of Hell. You will be coming to [enter] it. Had these [false deities] been [actual] gods, they would not have come to it, but all are eternal therein. For them therein is heavy sighing, and they therein will not hear. Indeed, those for whom the best [reward] has preceded from Us they are from it far removed." *{Anbiyā (21): 98-101}* Those shrines and tombs are idols even if they are ascribed to a pious friend of Allāh.

Specifying a Place for Making Vows:

Those gatherings which take place at shrines are from the celebrations of *Jāhiliyyah*, so whoever makes a vow there is disobedient and whoever attaches to this seeking nearness to the one in the grave, then the person is a *Mushrik*. The people within their contemporary *Jāhiliyyah* have begun to make vows to those who they believe in whether they be alive, dead or in shrines with money, clothes, animals, candles, incense, food and other items of property.

The people believe that their vows are a cause for gaining nearness to the pleasure of the one they seek the vow from and that the one who they are making a vow for has the ability to grant them their requests. If the people gain what they have asked for, this increases their attachment to those who they make vows to and intensifies their humility to them. The people will thus exert great efforts in placing their trust in them, even the Arabs of *Jāhiliyyah* attached less prestige to their idols than these people do today with their *Awliyā*...[1]

Al-Mīlī also said:

...this is what most of the common people have come to believe in with regards to those in the graves and those alive people known for piety and believing them to be able to that which only Allāh can do. This reached the extent that their tongues manifested what was in their hearts and they started to call upon them, at times along with Allāh and at other times by themselves, screaming out their names and glorifying them for possessing benefit and harm. The people are also humble towards them more than they are humble towards their Lord when making *salah* and *du'ā*.[2]

---

[1] Al-Mīlī, *Risālat ush-Shirk*, p.268

[2] Ibid.

Al-Mīlī also said:

The people consider touching (the graves) to be *tabarruk* (seeking blessings) for help *(istimdād)* from the souls of the dead pious, and they believe that they are alive in the graves, have an influence in the world and can grant the requests made to them. The people also build shrines on the graves of the dead pious and believe that the spirit of the righteous person is in the grave. You will actually find that there are great constructions built upon shrines ascribed to Shaykh 'AbdulQādir al-Jīlānī ﷺ who is buried in Baghdad!? While he ﷺ never even knew that place and never heard of it! You will find these shrines dedicated to Jīlānī in Western Algeria but most are in the East. In some cases we know that a dead person in a grave is not even righteous and the most famous of these types of people in our country is Shaykh Muhammad bin 'AbdurRahmān the founder of the *Rahmāniyyah* Sufi cult in our Maghrib. From what is associated with it is *tabarruk* for help *(istimdād)* along with kissing and touching the walls of the shrine and other things which are associated with the place (shrine).[1]

Ibn 'Āshūr said about the danger of *shirk*:

The greatest enmity is that which is done to the one who is rightfully to be ascribed with Magnitude because it is from His right that He

---

[1] Ibid., p.244

be singled out in worship in belief, actions and speech because that is His right upon the creation. It is mentioned in the hadeeth: *"The right of Allāh upon the servants is that they worship Him and not associate anything in worship with Him."*[1]

Then he said:

That is because shirk combines between accepting Allāh's Divinity and also accepting other than Him as having *Rubūbiyyah* also. So just as accepting other than Him is *dhulm*, their *īmān* in Allāh is also mixed with *dhulm*.[2]

---

[1] Reported by al-Bukhārī in *Kitāb ut-Tawheed* in the chapter *'Bābmā jā' fee Dua'a an-nabi Ummatuhu ila tawheedillāh'*, vol.13, p.347, *hadeeth* no.7373 from the *hadeeth* of Mu'ādh bin Jabal ﷺ.

[2] *At-Tahreer wa't-Tanweer*, vol.7, pp.332-333

[TN] It is worth us noting here the efforts of Shaykh 'Uthmān Ibn Fūdī (aka 'Dan Fodio'):

He is Abū Muhammad 'Uthmān ibn Muhammad ibn Fūdī, born in Marratta in northern Nigeria in 1168 AH/ 1754 CE. The name 'Dan Fodio' is the Hausa rendition of Ibn Fūdī. He was from a family of scholars that migrated to Hausaland from Futa Toro before the 15th century CE, bringing with it the Islamic tradition of Timbuktu. He waged a *jihād* in 1217 AH/1802 CE against clans that had violently opposed Islām and strongly repressed the Muslims. He established the Sokoto Islamic state which ruled by *Sharee'ah* in West Africa. He is known for his *tajdeed* efforts and his stance against innovations. A number of folkloric legends and myths surrounded the personality of Dan Fodio as some people claimed that he could "walk on water" or appear in dreams. Some people even claimed that he was *the Mahdi*! All of these ideas were refuted by Dan Fodio himself during his time. In a book entitled *Tanbīh ul-Faheem*, Dan Fodio refuted the claims of a man named Hammā who lived in Maganga, Nigeria and was claiming to be the *Mahdi*. The man was later executed for his heresy (MA al-Hajj, *The Mahdist Tradition in Northern Nigeria*, A.B.U. 1973). Dan Fodio however did make some comments in some of his works that were in line with the Ash'arīs, but at times he clearly said things in line with the *Salaf* (pious predecessors) He therefore was akin to Imām an-Nawawī and Ibn Hajar, who also had teachers that were of the Ash'arī *'aqeedah* but were not pure Ash'arīs.

Dan Fodio's chain of scholars however reveals interesting facts. One of his teachers was Jibreel ibn 'Umar of the Tuareg tribe who had made Hajj and thus lived in Makkah for a while. In Madeenah, Jibreel Ibn 'Umar studied with Muhammad Murtada az-Zabīdī (1145-1205 AH/ 1732-1791 CE) who was originally from India but had travelled to az-Zabeed in Yemen where he lived for a while and studied before going on to teach in Madeenah himself. One of az-Zabeedī's teachers was Shāh Waliullāh ad-Dehlawī (1702 – 1762 CE) of Delhi in India. Dan Fodio's uncle who taught him *hadeeth* was Muhammad bin Rāj who had studied under Abu'l-Hasan as-Sindī also from India and a teacher of *hadeeth* in Madeenah. Abu'l-Hasan as-Sindī was a student of Muhammad Hayāt as-Sindī another great *hadeeth* scholar of India who was also teaching in Madeenah. One of Muhammad Hayāt as-Sindī's students was Muhammad ibn Abdul-Wahhāb ﷺ. Also see a recent study conducted in Nigeria and written in Arabic entitled *Asānid al-Faqeer ad-Da'īf al-Mutashāfī bi'l-Mushaffa' Ahmad as-Shareef* (Ms. University of Ibadan Library 82/137: Ibadan, Centre of Islamic Documentation [CAD]). This *sanad* was also mentioned by an American Muslim researcher who had graduated from *MaDeenah University*. Also see the research of a non-Muslim researcher Stefan Reichmuth in his *"Murtada al-Zabidi (d. 1791) in Biographical and Autobiographical Accounts – Glimpses of Islamic Scholarship in the 18th Century CE"* in the Islamic studies journal *Die Welt Des Islams – International Journal for the Study of Modern Islam* (Leiden, Boston and Koln: Brill, Vol. 39, No. 1, March 1999) p.70. With regards to fanatical blind following of Imām Mālik, it is known that *"...the greatest contribution of Dan Fodio's reforming ideas, apart from his views on Sunnah and Bid'a, was in the field of madhāhib (schools of law)."* F.H. al-Misri (ed.), *Bayān Wujoob ul-Hijrah 'ala'l-'Ibād* (Khartoum University Press and OUP, 1978 CE)

'Uthmān ibn Fūdī said in his book *Hidāyatut-Tullāb* (Zaria: Gaskiya Corporation, 1961), p.2: *Neither Allāh in His book, nor the Prophet in his Sunnah made it obligatory that one particular madhhab should be followed, nor did we hear any of the early scholars enjoining a person to follow one way. If they had done that, they would have committed a sin by not allowing people to act in accordance with ahadeeth which that particular way did not give weight to.*

Other statements from 'Uthmān ibn Fūdī can be found in his book *Hisn ul-Afhām min Juyūsh il-Awhām* [The Fortification of Understanding Against the Armies of Delusion], this book was translated into English as *Islam Against Illusions* (Quality Press, 1989) by Fazlur Rahman Siddiqi. In the book, 'Uthmān ibn Fūdī says of many 'scholars, *'If such a person is not aware of the Sunnah it is not permissible to follow him...He is simply a lunatic lost in his special state.'* (ibid. p.105 [Arabic text], p. 157 [Eng. Text])

'Uthmān ibn Fūdī also says in the same book, *'Some people are ignorant of the Sunnah, but they are anxious to emulate the practices of their Shaykh. If you speak to them about the Sunnah they will reply, "My Shaykh was doing this, my Shaykh was doing that," thus contradicting the clear and open Sunnah.'* (Ibid. p. 90 [Arabic text], p. 99 [Eng. Text]).

Under delusion number 35 Imām 'Uthmān states: *'There are people in this country who venerate stones and trees...they sacrifice animals for them symbolizing that the stones and trees are great, and they even pour flour-paste on them.'* He further stated: *'The one who indulges in such activities is considered a kāfir according to consensus.'*

Dr Siddiqi stated (ibid. pp.34-36): *'Since innovations and superstitions prevailed in all parts of the country, the common people as well as the Muslim scholars of that time were involved in un-Islamic practices and the whole society changed into a corrupt and demoralized society.'*

Hence, there was a situation which was exactly what was prevalent during the epoch of Imām Muhammad ibn 'AbdulWahhab, Dr Siddiqi continues

'At that time, Muslims were called Muslims only because they were born in the so-called "Muslim families" while their characters and practices were against Islam and its education. Their belief was that some trees and stones deserved respect and worship and that these could

provide them with the means of subsistence or bless them with a child...Muslims of that time had totally lost their Islamic identifications because of their pagan practices. Even for a Muslim, it was difficult to recognize his Muslim brother. Even the Ulama accused the Shaykh, but they were not sincere in their remarks against him. Their attitude to the Shaykh was not based on their sincerity, but it was the result of a conspiracy against the Shaykh by the Sultān.' Dr Siddiqi also states on page 175 of *Islam Against Illusions*: *'According to Muhammad Bello...the main purpose of his (Imām 'Uthmān's) sermons was to teach the people the fundamentals of Islam; preferably, the principles of tawheed, the other articles of faith and the essential duties of a Muslim towards Islam.'*

Muhammad Bello ؒ was the son of Imām 'Uthmān. Therefore, here alone we can see a radical departure in the emphasis of Imām 'Uthmān and the *Sufis* of the era, who refrain from calling to *tawheed* based on their claim that it causes division! Not to mention the fact that they are largely ignorant of it. 'Uthmān ibn Fūdī also made similar statements in his books *Irshād al-Ummah ilā Tayseer il-Milla* and *Tawqeef ul-Muslimeen*. See Ahmad Mohammad Khani, *The Intellectual Origin of the Sokoto Jihad*, (Ibadan, Nigeria: Iman Publications, Muharram 1405 AH/1985 CE), pp.85-90.

It is also worth shedding some light on the Moroccan scholar and historian Abu'l-'Abbās Ahmad bin Khālid an-Nāsirī. He is Abu'l-'Abbās Ahmad bin Khālid bin Muhammad bin Muhammad bin Ahmad bin Muhammad an-Nāsirī and his lineage goes back to 'Abdullāh bin Ja'far bin Abee Tālib, husband of the sister of Hasan and Husayn ؒ. An-Nāsirī was from a family that was known for virtue and knowledge which had migrated to the city of Salā (Salè), near Rabat in Morocco in 1220 AH/1805 CE. He was born on Saturday 22 Dhu'l-Hijjah 1250 AH/March 1835 CE in Salā, which at that time was a city that was known for Islamic sciences, Arabic language and the study of Islamic texts. He studied the Qur'ān (Warsh 'an Nāfi') with al-Hajj Muhammad 'Alawī as-Salāwī and Muhammad bin Jīlānī al-Hāmidī. He also studied the works of ash-Shātibī, Ibn 'AbdulBarr, Ibn Mālik and Ibn Subkī with his cousin 'AbdusSalām bin Talhah. An-Nāsirī studied the sciences of the Arabic language with his teacher 'Allāmah Muhammad bin 'Abdul'Azeez as-Salāwī and studied a number of works on grammar, *balāghā* (rhetoric), logic, *fiqh* and *usūl ud-Deen*.

53

He was pivotal in disseminating knowledge, conducting research and benefiting the general masses of people in Morocco, excelling in historical works. He was also concerned with socio-religious issues moreso that most scholars of the time. He was very eloquent and as a result his lessons would be full and would have an effect on those present. He was strongly influenced by the *sunnah* in all affairs and strongly opposed the people of innovation and refuted them, exhorting them to refer back to the Qur'ān and *sunnah*. He opposed the leaders and sects of desires who had entered into the *Deen* that which was not from it, *'He also strongly safeguarded waking the Muslims from their heedlessness to the clear manhaj'*, (Biography by Ja'far and Muhammad an-Nāsirī, *Kitāb ul-Istiqsā' li-Akhbār Duwal al-Maghrib al-'Aqsā* [Dār ul-Baydā (Casablanca): Dār ul-Kitāb, 1954], vol.1, pp.14-15).

From his most correct and authentic books in particular are his historical *magnum opus, Tārīkh ul-Istiqs*ā' and *Ta'dheem ul-Minnah bi'n-Nasrati's-Sunnah* which according to Ja'far and Muhammad an-Nāsirī in their biography of him in the first volume of *Kitāb ul-Istiqsā'*, *'are filled with warning against this disease and these (false) opinions by paying attention to spreading authentic Islamic knowledge amongst the ummah and referring people to study from the books of the Salaf.'* He advised a number of governors in Morocco during his era on issues related to governance, economics and the *Deen*, he thus travelled to the cities of Tanger, al-'A'rāish (Larache), Marrākush (Marrakech), Dār ul-Baydā' (Casablanca), Salā (Sale), Tetwān (Tetoun), Ghumārah etc. initially he refused the posts as he thought that they would avert him from his scholastic efforts. He died on Thursday 16 Jumadā Ulā 1325 AH/12 October 1897 CE. He authored over thirty books (see ibid. pp.27-34) and his two main students were the jurist and author of Salā, al-Hajj Tayyib 'Awād and the historian Abū 'Abdullāh Muhammad bin 'Ali ad-Dakālee as-Salāwī. From the titles of the works that he authored, there is nothing whatsoever that shows that he was *Sūfī* and in fact the lengthy biography of him by Ja'far and Muhammad an-Nāsirī, there is no reference made whatsoever to Sufism. Furthermore, from the thirty works that he authored, none of the books have anything to do with Sufism, the contrary in fact, in the form of his books *Ta'dheem ul-Minnah bi'n-Nasrati's-Sunnah*. There may have been some members of his extended family and clan that were *Sūfīs*, but as for

Abu'l-'Abbās there is nothing to suggest that he was. Kurt S. Vikør in his book *Sufi and Scholar on the Desert Edge: Muhammad bin 'Ali al-Sanusi and his Brotherhood* (London: Hurst & Co., 1995) refers to Ahmad bin Khālid an-Nāsirī as being an historian and no where mentions him as being a *Sūfī*, and refers to others from the Nāsirī family as clearly being *Sūfīs*. An-Nāsirī died on 16 Jumadā al-Ulā 1315 AH/October 12 1897 CE, ﷺ.

In the eighth volume of *Kitāb ul-Istiqsā fi't-Tarikh al-Maghrib al-Aqsā*, a history of north-west Africa in nine volumes by an-Nāsirī ﷺ, he discussed at length the *da'wah* of Imām Muhammad ibn 'AbdulWahhāb. An-Nāsirī states that Sultān Sulaymān ibn Muhammad ibn 'Abdullāh al-Alawī (who succeeded his father as king of Morocco) was given the pledge of allegiance in Fez in 1226 AH/1811 CE was thus a contemporary of the Imām and scholar Sa'ud ibn 'Abdul'Azeez ibn Muhammad ibn Saud. Sultān Sulaymān wanted to closely examine the *da'wah* in Saudi and thus sent his son Abū Ishāq Ibrāheem (in 1226 AH/1811 CE) with a delegation of Moroccan scholars and notables with a letter from his father (Sulaymān). An-Nāsirī stated: *'Many among those who accompanied Ibrāheem during that Hajj trip told us that they did not witness any deviation in Islamic Law from Imām 'Abdullāh ibn Saud or his retinue. On the contrary, what they observed is steadfastness and care in performing the Islamic acts of worship, such as prayer, tahārah, fasting, forbidding evil and cleansing the Two Holy Sanctuaries of impure and evil practices that used to be committed therein without objection from anyone. When 'Abdullāh ibn Sa'ud met with Ibrāheem he showed him the type of respect due to members of the Prophet's family. Ibn Saud sat next to Ibrāheem as an acquaintance, among other things that Ibn Saud spoke about was that he asked the Moroccan delegation about this "People claim that we commit deviation from the Prophet's sunnah. What part of the sunnah did you see us contradict and what did you hear about us from people before we met?" Judge Abū Ishāq Ibrāheem az-Zadāgā, the (Moroccan) scholar who led the discussion with the Saudi Imām said "We heard that you say Allāh has settled on His throne in a humanly tangible manner that indicates His having a body." Abdullāh Ibn Saud responded, "We seek refuge in Allāh from this statement, we only repeat the statement of Imām Mālik ﷺ that 'Istiwā is known, the kayfiyyah (how) is unknown, asking about how it happened is an innovation and believing that istiwā occurred is an obligation.' Is anything wrong with this statement?" The judge said "No, this is also our belief."*

The judge then asked, "We were told that you deny that the Prophet and his brothers from the Prophets, peace be upon them, are alive in their graves?" When Ibn Sa'ud heard the Prophet's name he raised his voice reciting the prayers and peace upon him, saying "We seek refuge in Allāh from this idea too. We believe that he, and the rest of the Prophets, are alive in their graves, in a type of life that is above the life enjoyed by the martyrs"... See Shaykh Abu'l-'Abbās Ahmad bin Khālid an-Nāsirī, *tahqeeq* (verifying and checking) by Ja'far and Muhammad an-Nāsirī, *Kitāb ul-Istiqsā' li-Akhbār Duwal al-Maghrib al-'Aqsa* (Dār ul-Baydā' [Casablanca]: Dār ul-Kitāb, 1954), Vol.8, pp.121-122.)

An-Nāsirī then commented: '*I believe that Sultān Sulaymān believed in this too and this is why he wrote his famous treatise in which he criticized the extreme austerity of the Sufis who lived during his time and warned against abandoning the sunnah and excessive engagement in bida' (innovation). He also explained in his message the proper manner of visiting graves of righteous people and warned against excessive behaviour that commoners might commit at their vicinity as sincere advice to the Muslims, may Allāh increase him in goodness. Sultān Sulaymān also decided that a certain speech that emphasizes tawheed and rebukes bida' be recited in all Masājid where jumu'ah is held. He also instructed Sūfī zawiyas be closed down.*' See Shaykh Abu'l-'Abbās Ahmad bin Khālid an-Nāsirī, *tahqeeq* (verifying and checking) by Ja'far and Muhammad an-Nāsirī, *Kitāb ul-Istiqsā' li-Akhbār Duwal al-Maghrib al-'Aqsa* (Dār ul-Baydā' [Casablanca]: Dār ul-Kitāb, 1954), Vol.8, p.123.

In terms of the different prints of *Kitāb ul-Istiqsā'* then there is a more recent annotated edition by M. Hajji, B. Boutaleb & A. Tawfiq (Dār ul-Baydā' [Casablanca]: Mansurat Wizarat al-Taqafa wa-l-Ittisal, 2001-2005 CE) in 8 volumes. The oldest edition is the 1949 CE edition which is in nine volumes. A summarized edition was also published in three volumes in 1418 AH/1997 CE again by Dār ul-Kitāb in Casablanca and an-Nāsirī himself published it himself in four volumes in Cairo in 1894 CE. It was translated into French by the Orientalists Grauille in 1906 CE, G.S. Colin in 1923-25 CE, Fumey in 1934-36 CE. This first edition mentioned in this footnote is available from the library at *SOAS, University of London* and the ninth volume discusses the 'Alawī dynasty in Morocco.

⊰ Conclusion ⊱

All praise is due to Allāh who has made it easy and helped the completion of this, He alone has all blessings and virtue, and we have reached the results which can be concluded in the following;

1. The statements of the scholars of the past such as Mālik and his first companions with regards to *shirk* and its types and means are few due to the fact that the innovation of the grave-worshippers had not yet spread, rather they used to speak about some issues that were mentioned within the texts. This is opposed to the later Mālikī scholars who expanded upon these issues as is evident in the previous samples from their texts.

2. The *'Ulama* exerted great efforts in safeguarding *tawheed*, fighting against the innovation of the grave-worshippers and blocking the means to *shirk*.

3. The innovation of the grave-worshippers corrupted the beliefs of many people and led them to fall into major *shirk*.

4. The Divine Legislation explained the corruption of all means that lead to *shirk*, so the *Sharee'ah* prohibits all that has developed from the grave-worshippers which corrupt the beliefs of the Muslims.

5. *Shirk* humiliates a person because a person will worship another creation that is weak just like him. It also opens a door wide open to legends and superstitions.

To end this small effort I hope that the respected reader will excuse me for any shortcomings and I ask Allāh to make this work sincerely for His Noble Countenance and to grant us all success with the guidance of His Book and to traverse the *Sunnah* of His Messenger ﷺ.

Sufficient is Allāh for us and He is the Best disposer of affairs and our final du'ā is all praise is due to Allāh the Lord of the Worlds.

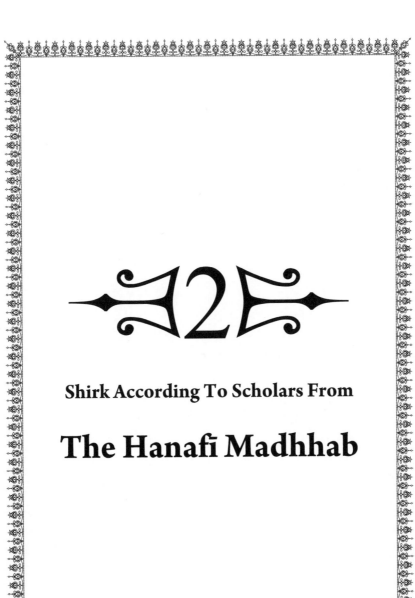

Shirk According To Scholars From

The Hanafi Madhhab

﹏ Introduction ﹏

The Hanafī 'Ulama are those who ascribe themselves to Abū Hanīfah in the branches of *fiqh* and they agree with him in the *Usool* in refuting the people of innovation like the Qubūriyyah. They also have praise-worthy efforts in clarifying *shirk*, its types, its means and manifestations within some Islamic societies. With this then, they also embark on the same caravan as the Mālikī, Shāfi'ī, Hanbalī scholars who maintain *tawheed* and confront the innovation of the grave-worshippers and others in order to block the means to *shirk*. This indicates that some of those who attribute themselves to the *Hanafiyyah* exerted great effort in combating the innovation of *shirk* of the grave-worshippers just like the people of the other *madhāhib*. They thus have commendable efforts in defending the pure *'aqeedah* from *shirk*, innovation and giving *da'wah* to this. The followers of the Imāms Abū Haneefah, ash-Shāfi'ī, Mālik, Ahmad and others have exerted great effort in promoting *tawheed* and averting *shirk*. So the matter is not as some think that only the Hanbalī scholars combated innovation and the *shirk* of the Qubūriyyah and others. I have thus put forward the efforts of the Hanafī scholars so that there will be a proof against the innovators and their followers, inshā'Allāh. I will thus relay samples of the statements of the

Imāms of the Hanafis in defining *shirk*, its types and means and I have divided this topic into four areas of research:

1. Definition of *shirk* according to the Hanafī 'Ulama

2. Types of *shirk* according to the Hanafī 'Ulama

3. The means to *shirk* that the Hanafī 'Ulama have warned against in order to preserve Tawheed.

4. Samples of *shirk* that the Hanafī 'Ulama have explained.

I ask Allāh to bring benefit with this Book and to make it sincerely for His Countenance and accept it from me sufficient is Allāh for us and He is the Best Guardian, and our final du'ā is all praise is due to Allāh, the Lord of the Worlds.

ᣔ Definition of Shirk According to the Hanafi Scholars ᣖ

Before we proceed with explaining the meaning of *shirk* according to the Hanafi scholars, it is useful to clarify the meaning of *shirk* linguistically, so we note:

Shirk linguistically

Imām 'AbdulQādir ad-Dehlawī[1] said:

Shirk is when one believes that other than Allāh possesses an attribute for the Attributes of Allāh, such as saying "so-and-so knows everything" or a person believes that so-and-so does whatever he wants, or that so-and-so possesses (the ability to deliver) good or evil; or averts to other than Allāh glorification which is not befitting, except to Allāh, such as prostrating to a person or seeking a need from him or believes in him.[2]

From this definition, it becomes clear that *shirk* according to him includes associating partners with Allāh in His Actions and Attributes, or in the

---

[1] He is 'AbdulQādir bin 'AbdurRaheem al-'Umarī ad-Dehlawī al-Hanafī, one of the prominent scholars who died in 1230 AH. See *Nuzhat ul-Khawātir*, vol.7, pp.302-304.

[2] *Tawdeeh ul-Qur'ān*, vol.1, p.105 – in Urdu.

actions of His Servants. This is what Imām Muhammad Ismā'eel ad-Dehlawī[1] and Shaykh Abu'l-Hasan an-Nadwī said:

> *Shirk* does not just depend on people equating a person with Allāh without a difference, rather the reality of *shirk* is that a person comes with actions which are specific for Allāh in His *'Uloohiyyah* and performing them to a person, such as *sujūd*, slaughter, making vows, seeking help when in need, believing that he is present in every place, affirming actions in the universe to him – affirming all of this for him is *shirk* and makes a person a *Mushrik*.[2]

These definitions of *shirk* explicitly show that the Hanafī Imāms did not fall short in explaining *shirk* and defining it as just being in regards to *Rubūbiyyah*, rather as you see, they viewed directing worship to other than Allāh as being major *shirk*. This is the *shirk* that nullifies actions and Allāh does not accept this, this is the *shirk* about which Allāh said,

﴿وَلَقَدْ أُوحِيَ إِلَيْكَ وَإِلَى الَّذِينَ مِن قَبْلِكَ لَئِنْ أَشْرَكْتَ لَيَحْبَطَنَّ عَمَلُكَ وَلَتَكُونَنَّ مِنَ الْخَـــسِرِينَ﴾

---

[1] He is Muhammad Ismā'eel bin 'AbdulGhanī bin 'AbdulHaleem al-'Umarī ad-Dehlawī al-Hanafī. He was born in Delhi in 1193 AH and died in 1246 AH, of his works are *Taqwiyat ul-Imān* and *Tanweer ul-'Aynayn fī Ithbāt Raf' il-Yadayn*, and other books.

[2] *Taqwiyat ul-Imān*, pp.22-23 (Urdu vers.) and an-Nadwī, *Risālat ut-Tawheed*, pp.32-33

"And it was already revealed to you and to those before you that if you should associate [anything] with Allāh, your work would surely become worthless, and you would surely be among the losers." {az-Zumar (39): 65}

Allāh says,

﴿وَمَن يَرْتَدِدْ مِنكُمْ عَن دِينِهِ فَيَمُتْ وَهُوَ كَافِرٌ فَأُوْلَـئِكَ حَبِطَتْ أَعْمَـلُهُمْ فِي الدُّنْيَا وَالآَخِرَةِ﴾

"And whoever of you reverts from his religion [to disbelief] and dies while he is a disbeliever — for those, their deeds have become worthless in this world and the Hereafter..." {Baqarah (2): 217}

Allāh says,

﴿مَن يُشْرِكْ بِاللَّهِ فَقَدْ حَرَّمَ اللَّهُ عَلَيْهِ الْجَنَّةَ وَمَأْوَاهُ النَّارُ وَمَا لِلظَّـلِمِينَ مِنْ أَنصَارٍ﴾

"Indeed, he who associates others with Allāh — Allāh has forbidden him Paradise, and his refuge is the Fire. And there are not for the wrongdoers any helpers." {al-Mā'idah (5): 72}

And Allāh says,

﴿إِنَّ اللَّهَ لاَ يَغْفِرُ أَن يُشْرَكَ بِهِ وَيَغْفِرُ مَا دُونَ ذَلِكَ لِمَن يَشَاءُ﴾

"Indeed, Allāh does not forgive association with Him, but He forgives what is less than that for whom He wills."

{an-Nisā (4): 48}

The actions of the Mushrik are worthless and he will be from the losers, Paradise is prohibited to him and Allāh will never ever forgive him for *shirk*. All of these aspects and types that they mentioned and transmitted are major *shirk* which the Arabs of the past committed and still remains within this Ummah. Shaytān beautified these actions unto them and used proofs to justify such actions, as Allāh says,

﴿أَلَا لِلَّهِ الدِّينُ الْخَالِصُ وَالَّذِينَ اتَّخَذُواْ مِن دُونِهِ أَوْلِيَاءَ مَا نَعْبُدُهُمْ إِلَّا لِيُقَرِّبُونَا إِلَى اللَّهِ زُلْفَى﴾

"Unquestionably, for Allāh is the pure religion. And those who take protectors besides Him [say], 'We only worship them that they may bring us nearer to Allāh in position.'"

{az-Zumar (39): 3}

Allāh also says,

﴿وَيَعْبُدُونَ مِن دُونِ اللَّهِ مَا لَا يَضُرُّهُمْ وَلَا يَنفَعُهُمْ وَيَقُولُونَ هَـؤُلَاء شُفَعَاؤُنَا عِندَ اللَّهِ﴾

"And they worship other than Allāh that which neither harms them nor benefits them, and they say, 'These are our intercessors with Allāh'" *{Yūnus (10): 18}*

And within other verses, this is even though at that time they affirmed that Allāh was the Creator, the Provider, the Sustainer, the One who gives life and brings death, as Allāh relayed about them,

$$﴿وَلَئِن سَأَلْتَهُم مَّنْ خَلَقَ السَّمَـوَتِ وَالأَرْضَ لَيَقُولُنَّ اللَّهُ قُلِ الْحَمْدُ لِلَّهِ بَلْ أَكْثَرُهُمْ لاَ يَعْلَمُونَ﴾$$

"And if you asked them, 'Who created the heavens and earth?' They would surely say, 'Allāh.' Say, '[All] praise is [due] to Allāh'; but most of them do not know." *{Luqmān (31): 25}*

Look at this strange contradiction and misguidance! Allāh is the One who created the person and provided for him yet the person affirms this and worships other than Allāh?! Glory be to Allāh from what they associate in worship with Him. However, many of the ignorant people believe that *Tawheed Rubūbiyyah* is what is demanded in Islam and is sufficient, in this way it has become easy for them to fall into shirk in *Ulūhiyyah* and direct acts of worship to other than Allāh. Whether these acts of worship be *du'ā, istighātha* or something else, and they do not consider that the Prophet ﷺ said *"Du'ā is worship."*[1]

For this reason, falling into this type of *shirk* has been easy for many of the ignorant people and also due to the negligence of the people of knowledge and the deviation of some of those who attached themselves to knowledge of this issue. However, within the statements of the Hanafi scholars of the past is an explanation of the types of *shirk* in *'Ubūdiyyah* and *shirk* in the Attributes of Allāh. These Hanafi scholars did not restrict themselves to emphasising one type of *shirk* rather they mentioned all of it.

---

[1] Reported by Ahmad, vol.4, pp.267, 276 and 27; Abū Dāwūd, vol.2, p.161 in *'Bāb ud-Du'ā'*, hadeeth no.1479; at-Tirmidhī, hadeeth no.2969 in the chapter of the *tafseer* of *Sūrah Baqarah*, vol.5, p.374, hadeeth no.3247; chapter on *tafseer* of *Sūrah Mu'minūn*, vol.5, p.456, hadeeth no.3372, chapter on the virtue of *du'ā*; Ibn Mājah, vol.2, p.1258, hadeeth no.3828, chapter on the virtue of *du'ā*; Bukhārī, *Adab ul-Mufrad*, p.105; Ibn Abī Shaybah, *al-Musannaf*, vol.6, p.21, hadeeth no.29167, chapter on the virtue of *du'ā*; Ibn Hibbān, vol.2, p.124, hadeeth no.887; al-Bayhaqī, *Shu'b ul-Imān*, vol.2, p.37, hadeeth no.1105; al-Hākim, *al-Mustadrak*, vol.1, p.491 – he said that the hadeeth has a *saheeh isnad* and adh-Dhahabī agreed as did Ibn Jareer in *at-Taghyeer*, vol.24, pp.78-79. All of them relayed the hadeeth via Yasī' al-Kindī from an-Nu'mān bin Basheer in *marfū'* form.

ٵ Categories of Shirk According to The Hanafi Scholars ؏

When reviewing the aforementioned categories, it becomes evident to us that they are not restricted to only *Tawheed Rubūbiyyah* but rather include and enumerate, as will be explained, *shirk* in *'Ubūdiyyah (Ulūhiyyah)* and *shirk* in Allāh's Names and Attributes (*Asmā' was-Sifāt*), which is to apply something from Allāh's Attributes to one of the creation or to be over-zealous in respect to one of the creation to the extent of raising his status to a deity. Unto you are statements[1] of some of the Hanafi scholars in explaining the types and categories of shirk:

Imām Ahmad as-Sirhindī[2] stated:

---

[1] Pay attention that the categories of *shirk* that the Hanafi scholars mention are merely samples of practices of *shirk* that are found within some Islamic societies due to ignorance being widespread. There is no doubt that they exerted great efforts with what they outlined yet if they mentioned *shirk* in acts of worship generally along with the evidences that would have been better in my view, or that they explained the types of *shirk* in terms of the acts of worship wherein *shirk* takes place without restricting it to the actions that are mentioned (by some of the Hanafi scholars).

[2] He is Ahmad bin 'AbdulAhad as-Sirhindī al-Hanafī al-Māturīdī an-Naqshabandī, he authored *Bayān ul-'Aqā'id* which is in accordance with the *madhhab* of the *Māturīdiyyah* and also a work entitled *at-Tahdheeb* which is a *Sūfī* work. He also has a treatise affirming Prophethood which is a refutation of *Shī'ah*, he also has other works. He died

Shirk is split into two categories:

- First: shirk in *wājib ul-wujūd* (the necessary existence)
- Second: shirk in *'ibādah* (worship)

Imām Ahmad ar-Rūmī[1] and Shaykh Subhān Baksh al-Hindī stated when they mentioned six categories of *shirk*:

Shirk ut-Taqreeb which is worship to other than Allāh in order to gain closeness[2] (*taqarrub*) to Allāh.[3]

At-Tahānawī[1] stated a number of types of *shirk* including:

---

in 1034 AH at the Sirhind Madrasah and was buried there, for his biography see *Nuzhat ul-Khawātir*, vol.5, pp.43-55.

[1] He is Ahmad bin Muhammad al-Aqhasārī al-Hanafī who was also known as "ar-Rūmī" who was from the *'Ulama* of the Ottoman state, he also has authored a number of classifications and taught the *Shari'* sciences as well as giving *fatāwā*. He died in 1043 AH (1634 CE), for his biography see *Hidāyat ul-'Ārifeen*, vol.1, p.157 and *Mu'jam ul-Mu'allifeen*, vol.2, p.83.

[TN] Ar-Rūmī authored *Majālis ul-Abrār wa Masālik al-Akhyār wa Mahāyiq il-Bida' wa Maqāmi' il-Ashrār*. The book consists of 100 sessions (*majālis*) each starting with a hadeeth from al-Husayn bin Mas'ūd al-Baghawī's (d.516 AH/1122 CE) *Masābih us-Sunnah*. Subhān Baksh translated *Majālis ul-Abrār* into Urdu and this work is known as *Majālis ul-Abrār 'ala'l-Khazeenat il-Asrār*. This work spread *tawheed* in India and condemned *shirk*, grave worship and *tawassul* at graves before the works of Imām Muhammad bin 'AbdulWahhāb's works penetrated there.

[2] Based on the saying of Allāh, **"We only worship them that they may bring us nearer to Allāh in position."**{*az-Zumar (39): 3*}

[3] *Majālis ul-Abrār 'ala Khazeenat il-Asrār*, pp.150-152.

- Shirk in 'ibādah;[2]

- Shirk in obedience;[3]

- Shirk in *tasmiyah* (naming);[4]

---

[1] He is Muhammd bin 'Ali bin Hāmid bin Sābir al-Hanafī al-'Umarī at-Tahānawī who was a Mutakallim (a speculative rhetorical theologian), writer, *faqeeh* and Māturīdī. He lived before 1158 AH (1745 CE), for his biography see *Nuzhat ul-Khawātir*, vol.6, p.278 and *Mu'jam ul-Mu'aliffeen*, vol.11, p.47.

[2] Based on when Allāh says, **"And We certainly sent into every nation a messenger, [saying], 'Worship Allāh and avoid tāghūt.'"** *{an-Nahl (16): 36}* And when Allāh says, **"We had certainly sent Noah to his people, and he said, 'O my people, worship Allāh; you have no deity other than Him.'"** *{al-A'rāf (7): 59}* And when Allāh says, **"Do not make [as equal] with Allāh another deity and [thereby] become censured and forsaken."** *{al-Isrā (17): 22}* Meaning do not avert your worship to other than Allāh by worshipping other than Him.

[3] Based on when Allāh says, **"Did I not enjoin upon you, O children of Adam, that you not worship Satan – [for] indeed, he is to you a clear enemy –"** *{Yāseen (36): 60}* And Allāh says, **"O my father, do not worship Satan. Indeed Satan has ever been, to the Most Merciful, disobedient."** *{Maryam (19): 44}*

[4] It is possible that he intended here using other than Allāh's Name when slaughtering, for Allāh says, **"And do not eat of that upon which the name of Allāh has not been mentioned, for indeed, it is grave disobedience."** *{al-An'ām (6): 121}* And Allāh says, **"He has only forbidden to you dead animals, blood, the flesh of swine, and that which has been dedicated to other than Allāh."** *{al-Baqarah (2): 173}* Or it is possible that he intended naming children with names which indicate worship to other than Allāh such as 'AbdulHārith and 'Abdul'Uzza, Allāh says, **"But when He gives them a good [child], they ascribe partners to Him concerning that which He has given them."** *{al-A'rāf (7): 190}* Meaning: they set up partners to Allāh... So they either gave the child a name which indicates servitude to other than Allāh such as 'AbdulHārith, 'Abdul'Uzza, 'AbdulKa'bah

71

- Shirk in knowledge;[1]

- Shirk in *qudrah* (ability)[2].[3]

Imām Waleeullāh ad-Dehlawī[4] mentioned a number of categories of *shirk* such as:

- Shirk in sujūd;[5]

- Shirk in seeking help;[6]

- Shirk in vowing;[1]

---

or the likes, or they associated partners in worship with Allāh after Allāh blessed them with the child.

[1] Based on when Allāh says, **"[He is] Knower of the unseen, and He does not disclose His [knowledge of the] unseen to anyone..."** *{al-Jinn (72): 26}* And Allāh says, **"Say, "None in the heavens and earth knows the unseen except Allāh..."** *{an-Naml (27): 65}*

[2] As Allāh states, **"He said, 'Do they hear you when you supplicate? Or do they benefit you, or do they harm?'"** *{Shu'arā (26): 72-73}* And also Allāh says, **"Indeed, those you worship besides Allāh do not possess for you [the power of] provision."** *{al-'Ankabūt (29): 17}*

[3] *Kashshāf Istilahāt il-Funoon*, vol.4, pp.146-153.

[4] He is Ahmad Waleeullāh bin 'AbdurRaheem bin WajeehudDeen al-'Umarī ad-Dehlawī one of the scholars of the *Deen* who authored works such as *al-Fawz ul-Kabeer*, *al-Budūr ul-Bāzighah*, *Hujjatullāhi Bālighah* and many other woks. He died in 1176 AH in the city of Delhi, refer to *Nuzhat ul-Khawātir*, vol.6, p.398, no.415 for his biography.

[5] Based on when Allāh says, **"So prostrate to Allāh and worship [Him]."** *{an-Najm (53):62}*

[6] Based on when Allāh says, **"You alone we worship and You only we ask for help."** *{al-Fātihah (1): 5}* As is found in the saying of the Prophet ﷺ: *"If you seek help then seek Allāh's help."* Reported by Ahmad, at-Tirmidhī and others.

- Shirk in *tasmiyah* (naming);[2]

- Shirk in obedience in *tahreem* (prohibiting) and *tahleel* (legalising);[3]

- Shirk in slaughtering;[4]

- Shirk in swearing oaths[5];[1]

---

[1] Based on when Allāh says, **"They [are those who] fulfil [their] vows and fear a Day whose evil will be widespread."** *{al-Insān (76): 7}* See the speech of the Hanafī scholars regarding this in: the *Hāshiyat* of Ibn 'ĀbiDeen to *ar-Radd ul-Muhtār*, vol.2, p.439-440; *al-Ibdā fī Madār il-Ibtidā'*, p.189; *Kitāb Ziyārat ul-Qubūr*, p.29; *al-Majālis ul-Arba'*, p.14. Allāh also says, **"Then let them end their untidiness and fulfil their vows and perform tawāf around the ancient House."** *{al-Hajj (22): 29}* See *al-Bahr ur-Rā'iq*, vol.2, p.298 and *Rūh ul-Ma'ānī*, vol.17, p.313.

[2] This has been discussed prior along with the intent of this and the evidence against it.

[3] As is found in the saying of Allāh, **"They have taken their scholars and monks as lords besides Allāh, and [also] the Messiah, the son of Mary. And they were not commanded except to worship one God; there is no deity except Him. Exalted is He above whatever they associate with Him."** *{at-Tawbah (9): 31}* As is mentioned in the *tafseer* of this verse reported by at-Tirmidhī and others when the Prophet ﷺ asked 'Adi bin Hātim: *"Did they not forbid what Allāh had allowed and allow what Allāh had forbade and you followed them in all of that?"* Adi replied "Yes." The Prophet ﷺ responded: *"That was your worship of them."*

[4] The evidence is when Allāh says, **"Say, 'Indeed, my prayer, my rites of sacrifice, my living and my dying are for Allāh, Lord of the worlds.'"** *{al-An'ām (6): 162}* Just as when Allāh says, **"So pray to your Lord and sacrifice [to Him alone]."** *{al-Kawthar (108): 2}* For the statements of the Hanafī scholars in this regard refer to the book *Tuhfat ul-Fuqahā*, vol.3, p.67.

[5] This is when the one swearing the oath does it believing that the one upon whom he is swearing has some aspect of perfection or greatness which is only due to Allāh, or the one swearing the oath equates whom he is swearing to with Allāh. If this is not the case

- Shirk in pilgrimage for other than Allāh[2].[3]

Shah Muhammad Ismā'eel[4] mentioned a number of categories of *shirk* such as:

- Shirk in making du'ā to the *Awliyā* and seeking assistance from them;[5]

- Shirk by making vows and slaughter to the *Awliyā*;[6]

---

then the mere verbal swearing of an oath is minor *shirk* and does not expel one from the religion.

[1] Based on what the Prophet ﷺ said: *"Whoever swears by other than Allāh has committed kufr."* Reported by Abū Dāwūd, al-Hākim and Ahmad. And in another narration: *"Whoever swears by other than Allāh has committed shirk."*
There is a prohibition from Imām Abū Haneefah of swearing by other than Allāh, for Imām Abū Haneefah stated: **"Do not swear except by Allāh out of tawheed and sincerity."** See *Bidā'i us-Sanā'i'*, vol.3, p.8. Ibn Najm al-Hanafī stated about the one who swears by other than Allāh: *"Kufr is feared for the one who says 'I swear on my life' or 'I swear on your life'."* See *al-Bahr ur-Rā'iq*, vol.5, p.124. Also see the speech of the Hanafī scholars in *al-Fatāwā al-Hindiyyah*, vol.6, p.323-326 and *al-Bahr ur-Rā'iq*, vol.3, pp.88, vol.5, p.124.

[2] Based on when Allāh says, **"And [due] to Allāh from the people is a pilgrimage to the House – for whoever is able to find thereto a way."** *{Āli 'Imrān (3): 97}*

[3] *Hujjatullāhi Bālighah*, vol.1, p.183 and in the newer edition: vol.1, p.543; also see *al-Budoor al-Bāzighah*, vol.125, p.127.

[4] His biography has been mentioned previously.

[5] Based on when Allāh said, **"And do not invoke besides Allāh that which neither benefits you nor harms you, for if you did, then indeed you would be of the wrongdoers."** *{Yūnus (10): 106}* And when Allāh says, **[Remember] when you asked help of your Lord, and He answered you...** *{al-Anfāl (8): 9}* See *Rūh ul-Ma'ānī*, vol.11, p.98, vol.6, p.129.

[6] The evidences against this have been mentioned beforehand.

- Shirk in seeking assistance from the *Awliyā*;[1]

- Shirk in naming by ascribing children to the *Awliyā* with the meaning that they give other than Allāh, such as 'AbdunNabī ('Slave of the Prophet'), Hibbat 'Alī, Hibbat Husayn, Hibbat ul-Murshid, Hibbat ul-Madār, Hibbat Sālar and all of these names are given out of aspiring for calamities to be averted from them;[2]

- Swearing oaths to other than Allāh;[3]

- Sending a nail to other than Allāh in the name of a *Walī* from the *Awliyā* of Allāh;

- Binding to a son something tied to his leg in the name of a *Walī* from the *Awliyā* of Allāh;

- Prostrating to other than Allāh;[4]

- Believing in the unseen realm ('Ilm ul-Ghayb) other than Allāh;[5]

---

[1] The evidences against this have been mentioned beforehand.

[2] The evidences against this have been mentioned beforehand.

[3] The evidences against this have been mentioned beforehand.

[4] The evidences against this have been mentioned beforehand, see *al-Bahr ur-Rā'iq*, vol.5, p.124; *al-Marqāh*, vol.2, p.202 and *Rūh ul-Ma'ānī*, vol.17, p.213.

[5] The evidences against this have been mentioned beforehand, see the statements regarding the ruling on the one who claims to know the Unseen realm within the following Hanafi books: *al-Fatāwā al-Hindiyyah*, vol.6, pp.323-326 and *al-Bahr ur-Rā'iq*, vol.3, pp.88, vol.5, p.124.

- Affirming that other than Allāh controls the affairs...[1]

- ...all of that is shirk and makes a person become a *Mushrik*.[2]

Imām Muhammad bin Ismā'eel ad-Dehlawī mentioned a number of types of shirk in another instance:

- Shirk in knowledge;[3]

- Shirk in control of the affairs;[4]

- Shirk in worship;[5]

- Shirk in repeating any action.[6]

Shaykh an-Nadwī followed him in this and also sternly criticised the grave-worshippers.[7]

---

[1] The evidences against this have been mentioned beforehand, see the statements of the Hanafi scholars regarding this in *al-Bahr ur-Rā'iq*, vol.2, p.892; *Rūh ul-Ma'ānī*, vol.17, p.213 and *al-Ibdā'*, p.189.

[2] *Taqwiyat ul-Imān*, vol.19, p.21 (Urdu version) and an-Nadwī, *Risālat ut-Tawheed*, vol.25, p.33.

[3] Based on when Allāh says, **"He knows what is [presently] before them and what will be after them, and they encompass not a thing of His knowledge except for what He wills."** *{Baqarah (2): 255}*

[4] Based on when Allāh says, **"Say, [O Muhammad], 'Invoke those you claim [as deities] besides Allāh.' They do not possess an atom's weight [of ability] in the heavens or on the earth, and they do not have therein any partnership [with Him], nor is there for Him from among them any assistant. And intercession does not benefit with Him except for one whom He permits."** *{Saba (34): 22-23}*

[5] This has been discussed prior.

[6] *Radd ul-Ishrāk*, pp.16-17

[7] *Risālat u '-Tawheed*, pp.34-40

﷽ The Means to Shirk Which the Hanafi Scholars Have Cautioned Against ﷽

The Hanafi scholars have openly forbade the means to *shirk* such as plastering graves *(tajsees)*, building structures on them, decorating them, writing on them,[1] , taking them as *masājid*,[2] putting lights on them,[3] facing

---

[1] Based on what was reported by Abū Dāwūd, at-Tirmidhī and others from the *hadeeth* of Jābir ﷺ that the Messenger of Allāh ﷺ forbade that the graves should be plastered (made into permanent structures) and that they be written on. To know more about the position of the Hanafis refer to: *Badā'i us-Sanā'i*, vol.1, p.320; *Tuhfat ul-Fuqahā*, vol.2, p.256; *Tabyeen ul-Haqā'iq*, vol.1, p.264; *Hāshiyat Marāqī ul-Falāh wa Marāqī il-Falāh*, p.405 and *al-Ibdā'*, p.197.

[2] Based on the saying of the Prophet ﷺ *"Allāh cursed the yahūd and the nasārā because they took the graves of their prophets as Masājid."* The *hadeeth* is agreed upon. He ﷺ also said : *"Those before you used to take the graves of their Prophets as Masājid, do not take graves as Masājid! I forbid you from doing that!"* Reported by Muslim and others. To know more about the Hanafi position on this issue refer to: *Tabyeen ul-Haqā'iq*, vol.1, p.264; *Rūh ul-Ma'ānī*, vol.15, p.237; *al-Murqā fi Sharh al-Mishkāt*, vol.2, p.22; *al-Kawākib ud-Darārī* [Gleaming Stars], vol.1, p.316-317; al-Bar'awī, *Ziyārat ul-Qubūr*, p.29 and *al-Majālis ul-Arba'*, p.13.

[3] Based on the saying of the Prophet ﷺ *"Allāh has cursed women who visit graves, those who build masājid on them and those who erect lamps (over them)."* Reported by Ahmad, at-Tirmidhī and others. In order to know about the position of the Hanafi scholars refer to: *al-Kawākib ud-Darārī*, vol.1, p.317; *al-Ibdā'*, p.189; *Ziyārat ul-Qubūr*, p.29 and *al-Majāis ul-Arba'*, p.13.

them in prayer and *du'ā*,[1] taking them as places of festivity[2] and travelling to them.[3]

---

[1] Muslim and the others reported that the Prophet 🕌 said: *"Do not sit on graves and to not pray on them."* Abū Haneefah disliked facing the grave of the Prophet 🕌 when making *du'ā*, see: *at-Tawassul wa'l-Waseelah*, p.293; *Rooh ul-Ma'ānī*, vol.6, p.125; *Majma' al-Anhur fī Sharh Multaqā al-Abhur*, vol.1, p.313.

[2] Abū Dāwūd reported from Abū Hurayrah 🕌 in *marfū'* form that the Prophet 🕌 said: *"Do not make your homes as graveyards, do not make my grave as a place of festivity and send salutations upon me for your salutations reach me wherever you are."* In order to know the position of the Hanafis on this matter refer to *al-Ibdā'*, p.185.

[3] Ahmad reported from Abū Sa'eed who said: the Messenger of Allāh 🕌 said: *"It is not befitting (specifically) to travel to any masjid for Salāh except Masjid ul-Harām, my masjid and Masjid ul-Aqsā."*

⇥ Samples of Shirk Which the Hanafi Scholars Have Cautioned Against ⇤

After it has been explained that the *Mushrikeen* from the Arabs did not associate (in worship with Allāh) in *Rubūbiyyah,* but rather committed shirk in *Ulūhiyyah,* there matters which can be deemed as strange. I say: "strange" because there are many manifestations of *shirk* in *Rubūbiyyah* among individuals in the Islamic Ummah today.

Muhammad 'Alā'uddeen al-Haskafi[1] said about those who makes vows to other than Allāh:

> You should know that what many of those common people do by devoting themselves to the dead and taking money... for candles, oils and the likes to the tombs of the dead pious in order to gain nearness to them – then all of that is by consensus bātil and harām.[2]

Ibn 'ĀbdiDeen said in explaining this text:

---

[1] He is Muhammad bin 'Ali bin Muhammad al-Hasanī, well-known as 'Alā-uddeen al-Haskafi, a *Hanafī Muftī* from Damascus. He authored *ad-Durr al-Mukhtār fi Sharh Tanweer il-Absār, Ifādat ul-Anwār 'alā Usūl il-Manār.* He died in 1088 AH. See *Khulāsat ul-Athar,* vol.4, p.63-65 and *al-A'lām,* vol.6, p.294.

[2] *Ad-Durr ul-Mukhtār ma' Radd il-Muhtār,* vol.2, p.439

His statement: *"to gain nearness"* is like when one says 'O my master if you return my lost relative, or cure my sick relative or give me what I need then unto you is this piece of gold, silver, food, candle or oil'. As for his statement: *"then all of that is by consensus bātil and harām"* then this is based on the following: *"Making vows to the creation is not permissible because it is worship and worship is not to be directed to the creation and the one who the vow is being made to is dead and the dead do not possess anything."*[1]

Al-Alūsī said in describing those who seek help from other than Allāh and their connection to the dead to the extent that they perform some aspects of obedience to the dead such as making vows and the like:

In the saying of Allāh,

﴿إِنَّ الَّذِينَ تَدْعُونَ مِن دُونِ اللَّهِ لَن يَخْلُقُواْ ذُبَاباً﴾

"Those who you call upon other than Allāh cannot create even a fly..." {al-Hajj (22): 73}

It indicates a censure of those who go to extremes in terms of the *Awliyā* of Allāh, wherein they seek help from them at the onset of a calamity being heedless of Allāh. These (extremists) also make vows to the *Awliyā* and those who are 'intelligent' among them say *"These Awliyā are our means to Allāh and we just make vows to Allāh and*

---

[1] *Radd ul-Muhtār 'ala'ad-Durr il-Mukhtār*, vol.2, pp.449-450.

make the reward for that go to the Walī". It is apparent that their first claim is just the same as that of the those people who worship idols and said,

$$\text{﴿مَا نَعْبُدُهُمْ إِلَّا لِيُقَرِّبُونَا إِلَى اللَّهِ زُلْفَى﴾}$$

"We only worship them that they may bring us nearer to Allāh in position." *{az-Zumar (39): 3}*

As for their second claim then there is no harm in that as long as they do not seek their sick relatives to be cured or for their lost to be returned to them and the likes.

Muhammad bin Yahyā bin Muhammad al-Kandahalawī al-Hanafī[1] said: As for building *masājid* over graves and tombs then this resembles the *Yāhūd* who built *masājid* over the graves of their Prophets and seniors. Within this is venerating the dead and resembling the idol-worshippers. As for placing lights and candles over graves then this in itself is a waste of money which is forbidden based on Allāh's saying,

$$\text{﴿إِنَّ الْمُبَذِّرِينَ كَانُوا إِخْوَانَ الشَّيَاطِينِ وَكَانَ الشَّيْطَانُ لِرَبِّهِ كَفُورًا﴾}$$

---

[1] Muhammad Yahyā bin Muhammad bin Ismā'eel al-Kandahalawī al-Hanafī, he was a writer and scholar who was well grounded academically. From his works are *al-Kawākib ud-Darārī*, he died in the year 1334 AH. Refer to the edited introduction of the *Musannaf* of Ibn Abī Shaybah, vol.1, p.27 and *al-'Ināqeed ul-Ghāliyah*, p.47.

"Indeed, the wasteful are brothers of the devils, and ever has Satan been to his Lord ungrateful." *{al-Isrā (17): 27}*

It also resembles the *Yāhūd* who used to light the graves of their seniors with candles then venerate these graves and preoccupy themselves with that which is not of concern.[1]

Al-Alūsī al-Hanafī said:

I have seen those who allow what the ignorant do at the graves of the dead pious such as honouring graves, building tombstones over graves, lighting graves with candles, praying to graves, making *tawāf* around graves, kissing them, gathering by the graves at specific times and other practices. All of that is opposition to Allāh and His Messenger 🌸 and innovating in the *Deen* that which Allāh did not permit. It would suffice you to know the truth by following what the companions of the Messenger of Allāh 🌸 did with his grave 🌸. His grave is the most virtuous grave on the face of the earth; therefore you should stop at what the companions did when they visited his grave and gave salutations.[2]

Imām Walīullāh ad-Dehlawī said:

O reader, if you were to stop at the accuracy of what is said about the creeds of *Mushrikeen* and their practices, and then look at

---

[1] *Al-Kawākib ud-Darārī*, vol.1, pp.316-317

[2] *Rūh ul-Ma'ānī*, vol.15, p.239-240

superstitious people today, especially those who reside in the abodes of Islām, you should ask yourself: what is their perception of "al-Wilāyah" (closeness to Allāh)? Despite their belief in the *Awliyā* of the past they view that the *Awliyā* are present in our current time, even though this is impossible! They also believe in venerating graves and thus have been tested with different types of shirk, innovation and superstitious beliefs and so distortion and resembling (the disbelievers) became settled within them and penetrated their souls. This was to the extent that the ruling of the *Saheeh* hadeeth was applied to them *"You will surely follow the ways of those before you..."* It is therefore a calamity and a tribulation when a group of Muslims, in name, fall into this, may Allāh help us out of this. So to conclude, it is from the Mercy of Allāh that He sent the master of the Prophets Muhammad bin 'Abdillāh ﷺ to the Arabian Peninsula and instructed him to establish the upright *Deen* and argue with those sects of falsehood via the Qur'ān.[1]

He also said in *al-Budūr ul-Bāzighah*:

The Messenger of Allāh ﷺ spoke the truth when he said: *"You will surely follow the ways of those who came before you, handspan by handspan, armspan by armspan to the extent that if they were to enter into a lizard's hole you would follow them into it."* The companions

---

[1] *Al-Fawz ul-Kabeer*, p.26 and p.20 of the old print.

asked "(You mean) the *Yāhūd* and the *Nasāra* O Messenger of Allāh?" The Messenger of Allāh ﷺ replied *"Who else?"*[1] Do you not see that the polytheists of Makkah used to concede that Allāh exists, as Allāh says,

﴿وَلَئِن سَأَلْتَهُم مَّنْ خَلَقَ السَّمَـــوَتِ وَالأَرْضَ لَيَقُولُنَّ اللَّهُ﴾

"And if you ask them who created the heavens and the earth they would surely say 'Allāh'." *{Luqmān (31): 25}*

Yet this did not suffice them from associating partners with Allāh... The Sādiq ul-Masdūq (the truthful and trusted one, i.e. the Prophet) ﷺ said in what was reported by at-Tirmidhī from 'Adī bin Hātim that he said: I heard the Messenger of Allāh ﷺ read the verse,

﴿اتَّخَذُوا أَحْبَــرَهُمْ وَرُهْبَــنَهُمْ أَرْبَاباً مِّن دُونِ اللَّهِ وَالْمَسِيحَ ابْنَ مَرْيَمَ وَمَا أُمِرُوا إِلاَّ لِيَعْبُدُوا إِلَــهاً وَحِداً لاَّ إِلَــهَ إِلاَّ هُوَ سُبْحَـــنَهُ عَمَّا يُشْرِكُونَ﴾

"They have taken their scholars and monks as lords besides Allāh, and [also] the Messiah, the son of Mary. And they were not commanded except to worship one God; there is no deity

---

[1] Reported by al-Bukhārī, *Kitāb Ahādeeth ul-Anbiyā*, *'Chapter: What Has Been mentioned about Isrā'eel'*, vol.6, p.494, hadeeth no.3457, and *Kitāb ul-'Ilm*, *'Chapter: Following the Ways of the Jews and Christians'*; Saheeh Muslim, vol.4, p.2054, hadeeth no.2669 – both via 'Atā bin Yasār from Abī Sa'eed al-Khudrī.

except Him. Exalted is He above whatever they associate with Him." *{at-Tawbah (9): 31}*

(Then he ﷺ said:) *"They did not worship them but if they made lawful something for them they allowed it and if they prohibited anything for them they would prohibit it."[1]*

We know that *shirk* is not restricted to worship rather it can also be in this way...the Prophet ﷺ indicated that there would be people who name *khamr* (alcohol, or any type of intoxicant) by other than its name, and they will also name *zinā* (adultery or fornication) other than its name and then say "Allāh has not forbidden this in His Book so there is no problem in this". Do you not see the people who say that the intoxicant that is made from honey[2] and the likes is not *khamr* and then they make it *halāl*. Those are the people about whom the Prophet ﷺ spoke about. There are also a people who say that if a man has sexual intercourse with his son's slavegirl then that is *halāl* for him, do you not see those people that if it is said to them "leave the sayings of people as they can be right at time or wrong at

---

[1] *Kitāb ut-Tafseer ul-Qur'ān, 'Bāb Sūrah Tawbah'*, vol.5, p.218, hadeeth no.3095; Ibn Jareer in vol.10, p.114; al-Bayhaqī in *as-Sunan*, vol.10, p.116 – all of these narrations are via Mu'asb bin Sa'd from 'Adī bin Hātim, at-Tirmidhī said "the hadeeth is ghareeb."

[2] *Al-Bit'* is a strong wine that is made from honey and dates, there is also a hadeeth in Bukhārī and Muslim wherein the Prophet ﷺ stated: *"O mankind! The prohibition of khamr (wine) has been revealed and that is made of five things: Grapes, dates, wheat, barley and honey: and khamr what covers intellect."* [TN]

times and stick to the Book and what was reported by as-Sādiq al-
Masdūq 鑾," – they reply,

$$﴿إِنَّا وَجَدْنَآ ءَابَآءَنَا عَلَىٰ أُمَّةٍ وَإِنَّا عَلَىٰ ءَاثَـٰرِهِم مُّهْتَدُونَ﴾$$

**"Indeed, we found our fathers upon a religion, and we are, in
their footsteps, following."** *{az-Zukhruf (43): 23}*[1]

So they erred with this view and they are truly *Mushrikeen!*[2]

Imām Ismā'eel ad-Dehlawī said in his book *Tawiyat ul-Īmān* about the
fitna of *shirk* and ignorance among the people, and Abu'l-Hasan an-Nadwī
in his treatise on *tawheed* followed him, that:

(You should) know that shirk has become widespread among the
people during this era to the extent that sincere *tawheed* has become
strange. However, most of the people do not know the meaning of
shirk and claim that they have *Īmān* even though they are entrenched
in *shirk* and polluted by it. So what is important before anything is
for the people to fully comprehend the meaning of *shirk* and *tawheed*
and their rulings in the Qur'ān and hadeeth.

Manifestations of Shirk and its Various Types:
From what is witnessed today is that many people seek assistance
from Shaykhs, Prophets, Imāms,[1] martyrs, angels and jinn at the

[1] This is mentioned in the older print.
[2] *Al-Budūr al-Bāzighah*, pp.167-170

onset of calamities. They also call out their names and ask them their needs and ask them to fulfil their requests and make vows to them and seek nearness to them. They also ascribe their children to these (false deities) hoping for their requests to be given, as a result they name their children *"AbdunNabī", "'Ali Baksh", "Husayn Baksh", "Sālār Baksh"*. As for the Prophets and Messengers, then there is no problem in us holding them in great estimation and love but as for us putting them on the same level as Allāh and believing that they share the same status as Allāh then that is *shirk* and there is no doubt about this. However, we do not say this, rather we believe in the opposite - that the Prophets are of Allāh's creation and servants of Allāh. As for us believing that the Prophets have the ability to affect what goes on in the world then Allāh has not honoured them or characterised them with this. So they do not have a role in affecting what goes on in the world except with Allāh's Permission and Pleasure. So we neither call upon them nor seek help from them, for *du'ā* is unto Allāh and we seek help from Him alone.

---

[1] He intends by this the Imāms of Ahl ul-Bayt about whom the *Shī'a* exaggerated over and began to venerate and glorify, believing them to be infallible. The *Shī'a* also believe that their Imāms know the unseen realm of existence and they interpret "Imām" as sharing in Prophethood and as actually competing with Prophethood within many characteristics. Some people of the Sunnah in India have become affected by the beliefs of the Shī'a due to their rulers who mixed with them and were ignorant of Islām. This was stated by Abu'l-Hasan an-Nadwī.

There are people therefore who discard the Speech of Allāh and the statements of the Messenger of Allāh (ﷺ) and their views and allowed their shallow minds to accept that which is untenable. They also stubbornly attached themselves to legends and tales which cannot be traced historically or within authentic transmissions. They sufficed with superstitious *taqleed* and ignorant customs and if only they understood the Speech of Allāh and His Messenger they would have known that these were the same interpretations and proofs that were used by the kuffār Arabs during the time of the Prophet ﷺ and yet Allāh did not accept that from them, rather Allāh rejected that. Allāh says in Sūrat Yūnus,

$$﴿ وَيَعْبُدُونَ مِن دُونِ اللّهِ مَا لاَ يَضُرُّهُمْ وَلاَ يَنفَعُهُمْ وَيَقُولُونَ هَـؤُلاء شُفَعَاؤُنَا عِندَ اللّهِ﴾$$

"And they worship other than Allāh that which neither harms them nor benefits them, and they say, 'These are our intercessors with Allāh'." *{Yūnus (10): 18}*

So we know from this verse that there is none in the heavens and earth who can interceded for another, and whose intercession can benefit another, even the intercession of the Prophets, except with Allāh's permission,

$$﴿وَلاَ يَشْفَعُونَ إِلاَّ لِمَنِ ارْتَضَى وَهُم مِّنْ خَشْيَتِهِ مُشْفِقُونَ﴾$$

"...and they cannot intercede except on behalf of one whom He approves. And they, from fear of Him, are apprehensive." {al-Anbiyā (21): 28}

So even if someone calls upon them, or shouts out their names, or neither calls upon them nor shouts out their names, this will not be achieved except whatever Allāh wills and instructs.

The Reality of the Shirk of the People of Jahiliyyah and their Misguidance

Likewise, it is clear that the kuffār who were during the time of the Prophet ﷺ did not equalise their deities with Allāh or view their gods as being on the same level as Allāh. Rather they used to affirm that their objects of worship were from the creation of Allāh and did not at all believe that their gods had ability or power over Allāh or shared the same status as Allāh. Their *kufr* and *shirk* was by their calling upon their gods, making vows to them, gaining nearness to them by mentioning their names, taking them as intercessors. So whoever treats anyone as how did the kuffār (Arabs) did with their gods, even if he affirms that they are created and slaves (of Allāh), has the same position as Abū Jahl did in terms of shirk.

The Harms of Shirk and its Practises:

Know that *shirk* does not just stop at a person making someone equal with Allāh and viewing them as being the same with no difference, rather the reality of *shirk* is manifest when a person performs actions that are specifically for Allāh and His Elevated Self, and are symbols of servitude to Allāh, and directs them to a person, such as: *sujūd* to someone, slaughtering in the name of someone, making vows to someone, seeking help by someone at the onset of a calamity, believing that a person is omnipresent everywhere (*hādhir nādhir*), affirming that a person has the ability to control within (the world) – all of that confirms shirk and deems a person a Mushrik. This is even if the person believes that this person, angel or jinn that is prostrated to, slaughtered to, vowed to or sought help from is less in status than Allāh and affirms that Allāh is the Creator while the object (to whom these practices of worship are dedicated) is a servant and creation (of Allāh). And there is no difference in this between Prophets, *Awliyā*, *jinn, Shayāteen*, powerful *jinn (*'afāreet*)* – whoever treats these with such actions and practices of worship is a Mushrik. For that reason Allāh described the *Yāhūd* and the *Nasārā*, who went to extremes with their priests and Rabbis, just as the *Mushrikeen* went to extremes with their deities, and Allāh became angered with them as He did with the Mushrikeen, Allāh says,

﴿اتَّخَذُواْ أَحْبَــرَهُمْ وَرُهْبَــنَهُمْ أَرْبَاباً مِّن دُونِ اللَّهِ وَالْمَسِيحَ ابْنَ مَرْيَمَ وَمَآ أُمِرُواْ

إِلاَّ لِيَعْبُدُواْ إِلَــهاً وَحِداً لاَّ إِلَــهَ إِلاَّ هُوَ سُبْحَــنَهُ عَمَّا يُشْرِكُونَ ﴾

"They have taken their scholars and monks as lords besides Allāh, and [also] the Messiah, the son of Mary. And they were not commanded except to worship one God; there is no deity except Him. Exalted is He above whatever they associate with Him." *{at-Tawbah (9): 31}*

Allāh also mentioned that all of creation, be they *'Ulama,* worshippers, rulers or kings are all humble servants, weak and incapable, they do not possess the power to grant life or death or to resurrect. They do not possess anything if Allāh sends for them and asks them to stand in front of Him out of humility, submissiveness and obedience. Allāh says,

$$﴿إِن كُلُّ مَن فِى السَّمَـوَتِ وَالْأَرْضِ إِلاَّ آتِى الرَّحْمَـنِ عَبْداً - لَّقَدْ أَحْصَـهُمْ وَعَدَّهُمْ عَدّاً - وَكُلُّهُمْ ءَاتِيهِ يَوْمَ الْقِيَـمَةِ فَرْداً ﴾$$

"There is no one in the heavens and earth but that he comes to the Most Merciful as a servant. He has enumerated them and counted them a [full] counting. And all of them are coming to Him on the Day of Resurrection alone."n*{Maryam (19): 93-95}*

So it is apparent that only He (Allāh) has control and that none other than Him possess control within the universe and people will go to their Lord alone and none will be able to avert this, the verses of the Qur'ān which mention this are many.

Whoever contemplates on the verses which we have highlighted, and upon other verses, will know that there is a difference between *shirk* and *tawheed* and their realities are well known. The time has now come for us to mention some actions which Allāh specified for His Exalted Self and did not permit for others to partake in. There are many actions and to mention them would be lengthy, however we have to mention that of them that we are able to for the benefit of the reader who has intelligent understand that distinguishes truth from falsehood and guidance from misguidance.

All-Encompassing Knowledge is a Characteristic of Allāh

In introducing these matters, it is important to know that it is from Allāh's affair that in terms of knowledge, only He is present and aware of everything, knowing every detail, whether it is far, hidden or apparent. Nothing is hidden from Him at any time between the night and day, between the heavens and the earth, between the mountain tops and the waves of the sea, this knowledge encompasses all times and places and even an atom's weight does not escape Him,[1] this is a characteristic particular to Allāh, no one else shares in this with Him. So whoever constantly praises anyone from the creation and calls out to him while standing or sitting, whether near or far,

---

[1] [TN]: Allāh says, **"Not absent from Him is an atom's weight within the heavens or within the earth or [what is] smaller than that or greater, except that it is in a clear register..."** {*Saba (34): 3*}

and shouts out to him and seeks help form him at the onset of calamities, or calls on him to repel enemies, and ends by mentioning his name and focuses his mind on him, and directs his concerns to him, forming his image in his mind as if he can see him, and believes that by mentioning his name with his tongue or heart, or imagining him, or imagining his grave, and believes that he knows about that, and believes that nothing is hidden from him, and believes that he can deliver illness and good health, difficulty and ease, life and death, grief and happiness – then with these (beliefs) the person is a Mushrik and all of these actions are deemed as *shirk*. This type of *shirk* is branded as *Ishrāk fi'l-'Ilm* [Association in Knowledge] and it is to affirm the Divine Attribute of All-Encompassing Knowledge to other than Allāh. This is even if such affirmation is given to a Prophet, a Walī, a Shaykh, a martyr, an Imām,[1] a descendent of an Imām, an *'Ifreet* or a *jinn*. This is whether the person believes that he knows from his own self or believes that Allāh has granted him this knowledge and has become an attribute of his which is not to be removed – then all of that is *shirk*.

<u>Absolute Control of Affairs as He Wills and Perfect Ability are from the Characteristics of Allāh</u>

---

[1] Meaning the Imams of the Ahl ul-Bayt, as stated by Shaykh Abu'l-Hasan an-Nadwī.

The second thing which a person has to believe in is: that controlling the world with will and performing commands and prohibitions, and giving life and death, and giving and withholding provision, and granting good health or illness, and giving victory or defeat, and subjecting the Divine Decree on a person so that he is either always aided and successful or a failure, and granting requests and fulfilling hopes, and repelling calamities, and helping at times of difficulty – all of these are from the special characteristics of Allāh and no one shares in them whether they be Prophets, *Awliyā, Shuhadā'* (martyrs), righteous, *'afāreet* or *jinn*. Whoever affirms these characteristics of controlling the universe to anyone other than Allāh and seeks his needs from them, and seeks nearness to them and makes vows to them, and makes *istikhārah* to them – is a *Mushrik*. This type of *shirk* is called *Ishrāk fi't-Tasarruf*. Whether a person believes that those other than Allāh can do this from their own accord or believes that Allāh has given them this ability.

ACTIONS OF WORSHIP AND ITS SYMBOLS ARE PARTICULAR TO ALLĀH

The third thing is that Allāh has specified actions of glorification to Himself: these are called *"ibādah"* (acts of worship) and include: *sujūd* (prostration), *rukū'* (bowing), standing in humility (like placing the right hand over the left),[1] giving money in the name of the one who he believes is righteous or infallible, fasting for him, travelling to visit his sanctuary from faraway distances, making pilgrimage to his sanctuary (or tomb), calling out his name while en route to his sanctuary like the *talbiyah*, staying away from filth, sin and hunting animals, holding great reverence to these practices, making *tawāf* around his sanctuary, prostrating to it, making vows by it, covering the sanctuary just as the Ka'bah is covered, making *du'ā* by it, seeking help by it, asking for worldly needs, and needs of the hereafter, to be fulfilled, and for hopes to be fulfilled, and kissing a stone from the stones of this sanctuary and touching its walls, and touching its cover, and lighting the place with candles around it out of veneration and worship, and performing rites for it as its custodians do, providing beds and water for the pilgrims, and drinking water at its well for blessings, and pouring such water over the body, distributing such water to people, carrying it to those who were not present, walking backwards so as not to show the backside to the sanctuary, and respecting all that surrounds the sanctuary and not killing game that is near the sanctuary, not cutting down trees

---

[1] Like a servant does in front of his masters when in the company of kings, as is done in the non-Arab lands – as stated by Abu'l-Hasan an-Nadwī. I say: from this is also what we see often with the ignorant grave-worshippers at the Masjid of the Prophet 🌸 where one will place his right over his left standing in humility facing the noble grave with more fear and humility than he would be in front of Allāh in Salāh.

95

near the sanctuary (or tomb) – all of these actions Allāh has taught to His servants and Allāh has singled out these actions for Himself alone.

So whoever directs these actions of worship to a Shaykh of a (Sūfi) *tareeqah*, to a Prophet, a jinn a grave or a place of worship, or to an artefact of a righteous person and seeks blessing from such artefacts or to symbols that the pious person was known for, or prostrates to a coffin or bows to a coffin, or fasts in the name of a dead pious person[1] or stands in front of him out of awe and humility placing one of his hands over the other, travelling to a faraway sanctuary, lighting candles by them out of reverence and worship, or covering the sanctuary with a cover (like how the Ka'bah is covered), or placing a curtain over the tomb,[2] or kissing the grave,[1] or using a fan

---

[1] It is apparent that the innovation of fasting in the name of dead pious men or women from the Muslim Ummah emerged in the past within India. This fasting can even be for people who have no actual existence yet this fasting has its own regulations and specified days wherein people seek their needs from the dead pious person in whose name they fast. Imām Shaykh Ahmad bin 'AbdulAhad as-Sirhindī (d. 1034 AH) criticised this in one of his letters to one of the righteous women of his time who was followed and to whom such acts of worship were directed. He branded such actions as *shirk* in *'ibādah*, *Risālat* no.3, p.41 from the *Rasā'il* [Treatises] of Imām Ahmad bin 'AbdulAhad as-Sirhindī, as stated by Abu'l-Hasan an-Nadwī.

[2] Abu'l-Hasan an-Nadwī stated that the extremists in their praise and veneration of the dead and tombs go to the extent of covering tombs of the Awliyā and dead pious with coverings and cloth and treat them as they would treat a living Shaykh or great person.

on the grave to keep the flies of, just as servants do with their masters, or placing a pavilion over the tomb, or kissing its steps, or sitting on the tomb, and respecting all the trees, plants and herbs which surround the tomb and not dishonouring them – all of such actions are deemed as *shirk* and are entitled *Ishrāk fi'l-'Ibādah*. Whether a person believes that these things are venerated in themselves or that Allāh will be pleased with such actions (to other than Him) when it is only Allāh who avert disasters when such actions of worship are performed.

Signs of Glorification Which Indicate Servitude and Submission are Specifically for Allāh

Fourthly: Allāh taught His servants ways to straighten their *īmān*, bring about blessings in their worldly lives and achieve their needs. Such as by making vows to Allāh at the onset of calamities, calling

---

These innovations emerged in some Arab lands and Shaykh 'Ali Mahfūdh al-Hanafi says in his book *al-Ibdā' fi Madār il-Ibtidā'*: '*Shaytān beautified to these people serving tombs in order to open up for them filthy provisions, so you will see that when any of them (custodians of such tombs) needs to change the cover of the coffin each year they deceive the common people into thinking that the cover is blessed and can cure the sick, prevent envy and bring about wealth and safety from all plans and fears. The simple people have given in to these things and they have begun to waste a lot of money in such practices in order to easily gain more money.*' *Al-Ibdā*, pp.96-97

[1] This is from the customs of the extremists and the ignoramuses in India, as stated by Abu'l-Hasan an-Nadwī.

97

out with His Name at times of difficulty, beginning all acts in His Name, slaughtering for Him when one has been provided with a child and naming the children with names which highlight tawheed and servitude such as *"Abdullāh", "AbdurRahmān", "Hibbatullāh", "Jādul-Mawla", "Atāullāh", "Atiyyaullāh", "Amatullāh", "AtiyyaturRahmān".*[1] And they also specify a portion of farmland and orchads to the name of Allāh and dedicate some wealth. They should also believe that all that afflicts them from good and evil, famine, poverty and wealth, good health and sickness, victory and determination, happiness and satisfaction, good fortune, grief and joy – is all in the control of Allāh and goes back to Allāh's Mashee'ah (Will) before His Irādah (Desire).

So one should say "I will do such-and-such if Allāh wills" hereby glorifying His name which indicates His Ability and the inability of the servant of Allāh. So for example one says *"O my Lord", "O my Master", "O my Creator"* and if one wants to swear an oath then that should be done in His Name – and there are other signs and symbols of glorification. Whoever directs these acts of worship to the Prophets, *Awliyā, Shuhadā', 'Afāreet* or *jinn* (has committed Shirk),

---

[1] The author mentions here Indian names which include tawheed and highlight the correct 'aqeedah such as "Khuda Baksh" which means "Hibbatullāh" and "Allāh Diyā" which means "'Atiyyatullāh". We have changed the names to those names which are widespread within the Arab lands in order to make it easier for the Arabic reader to understand the intent, as stated by Abu'l-Hasan an-Nadwī.

and for example, makes vows to them at calamities, or calls out their names when sick, or uses their names for their children when provided with a child, and makes vows to them or names his children with names like *"AbdunNabī"*, "Imām Bakhsh" and *"Pīr Bakhsh"* and specifies part of the produce of one's farm or orchard to its name and presenting the cultivation and fruits that the earth has cultivated to those (false deities) and then using some for one's own needs then dedicating wealth and cattle to these false deities and respecting the animals by not removing them from fodder and straw and not beating them with sticks or stones; observing past customs and common traditions of food, drink and clothing and adhering to these customs just as one would adhere to the regulations of the Sharee'ah; and prohibiting food and clothing to people (such as between males and females, so it is said for example that men should not near such-and-such a food)[1] and that concubines should not go near certain food or that a woman who has been married twice should not go near certain foods and that *khabees* that has been prepared in the name of Shaykh 'AbdulHaq[2] is not to be eaten by

---

[1] A type of food that is cooked in India in the name of Sayyidah Fātimah ☙, the daughter of the Prophet ﷺ and men are forbidden from eating this food and only women can eat it, so men stay away from eat – as stated by Abu'l-Hasan an-Nadwī.

[2] Meaning Shaykh 'AbdulHaq ad-Dehlawī who was form the senior Shaykhs, teachers and Imams of the *Chisti Sūfi tareeqah* (cult) in India. He was born in Ridwali which is

whoever has used a *nārjeelah*;[1] and that whatever good or bad happens, or whatever calamity or prosperity occurs, is ascribed to those Shaykhs and *Awliyā*. So the person begins to say "such-and-such came across so-and-so and cursed him then he became mad" "so-and-so was rejected by so-and-so and then he became poor", "so-and-so blessed so-and-so and helped him to have good fortune". Or the person says "If Allāh, His Messenger and so-and-so want" or says "If my Shaykh wants, such-and-such will happen" or he ascribes to the one who he praises attributes which are specifically for Allāh and which are descriptions of glory and magnificence, which indicate: no need of the creation, absolute power, unlimited generosity which is only for the one worthy of worship, the richest of the rich, the God of gods, the Possessor of the possessors and the King of kings. Or a person may swear an oath by the Prophet, by 'Ali or by one of his

---

near Lucknow, he emphasised tawheed, the implementation of the Sharee'ah, preserving the obligations and *Sunan* and calling the people to Allāh. He died in 836 AH and after he died the extremists and ignoramuses in India invented a number of practices dedicated to him such as preparing a special food which has strict rules that are adhered which is named "Zād Shaykh 'AbdulHaq" it is made from semolina and sugar.

[1] Meaning a *sheeshah*, as stated by Abu'l-Hasan an-Nadwī. Khabees is: a mixed sweet –as stated by Abu'l-Hasan an-Nadwī.

[TN]: Khabees is a sweet that is popular in the Persian Gulf region and is like a pudding or jelly that is served for breakfast mainly at 'Eid times. It is made from butter, honey, dates and starch. Nārjeelah, sometimes spelt "narjileh" is commonly used in Shām (i.e. Greater Syria: Jordan, Lebanon, Palestine and Syria).

descendents (who the Imāmi Shī'a brand as being the "Twelve Imāms"), or by a Shaykh or by a grave – then all of that is deemed as shirk and is named Ishrāk fi'l-'Ibādah meaning that other than Allāh is glorified with certain actions and practices which are only befitting to be directed to Allāh. These four types of shirk have clearly been mentioned in the Qur'ān and hadeeth.[1]

After these samples have been mentioned by the Hanafī 'Ulama to explain that shirk is present within this Ummah, it will become clear to you that this refutes the saying of those who claim that major shirk will not possibly emerge among the Ummah of Muhammad ﷺ. It is evident to all who have a soul that many shades of shirk appeared within the Ummah of Muhammad ﷺ and are manifest. The saying of the Prophet ﷺ is sufficient as an evidence: *"The hour will not be established until tribes from my Ummah will follow the Mushrikeen and until some tribes from my Ummah will actually worship idols."*[2] And in another wording: *"...until groups from my Ummah will worship idols."* The Prophet ﷺ said: *"The Hour will not be established until the buttocks of the women of Daws move around Dhu'l-Khalasah (an idol*

---

[1] *Risālat ut-Tawheed*, pp.25-44

[2] Reported by Abū Dāwūd, *Kitāb ul-Fitan, 'Bāb Dhikr ul-Fitan wa Dalāilihā'*, hadeeth no.4252, its basis in Muslim, vol.4, p.2215 and al-Albānī mentioned it in *Tahdheer us-Sājid*, p.120.

which was worshipped by the tribe of Daws during the period of Jāhiliyyah)."[1] He also said 鑿: *"The night and day will not depart until al-Lāt and al-'Uzza are worshipped."*[2]

These matters mentioned in the *ahādeeth*, even if they have not yet occurred exactly has mentioned, are still no doubt a reality. However, what has emerged within the Ummah is worship of the creation such as (worship of) *Awliyā'* and others and directing acts of worship to them such as slaughtering, making vows, supplicating and seeking assistance and other acts of worship – this is major *shirk* and is not denied except by a rejecter. The Prophet 鑿 warned from *shirk* that most people do not pay any concern to wherein he said: *"O people fear the shirk which is more hidden than the crawling ant."*[3] So if it is said:

---

[1] Reported by Bukhārī in *Kitāb ul-Fitan, Taghyeer az-Zamān hatta Tu'bad al-Awthān*, vol.13, p.76, *hadeeth* no.7116; Saheeh Muslim, *Kitāb ul-Fitan, La Taqūm as-Sā'h hatta Ta'bud Daws Dha'l-Khalasah*, vol.4, p.2230, *hadeeth* no.2906. Both *hadeeth* are via Sa'eed Ibn Musayyib *(rahimahullāh)* from Abū Hurayrah 鑿.

[TN]: 'Daws' are a tribe originally from Yemen and Dhu'l-Khalasah was a house full of idols and named 'Dhu'l-Khalasah' because it was believed that whoever made *tawāf* around it would achieve 'khallasa' (purity). The *hadeeth* proves that Daws will apostate from Islām and return to *shirk* to the extent that their women will go around the idol with their rear-ends wiggling about around it.

[2] Relayed by Muslim in *Kitāb ul-Fitan wa Ashrāt is-Sa'ah*, vol.4, p.2230, *hadeeth* no.2907 via Abū Salamah from Ā'ishah *(radi Allāhu anhumā)*.

[3] Reported by Ahmad in *al-Musnad*, vol.4, p.403; Ibn Abī Shaybah in *al-Musannaf*, vol.6, pp.70-71, *hadeeth* no.29547 in the chapter of *Ta'ūdh min ash-Shirk*; Bukhārī in

"How can a person who accepts the Creator, the Day of Judgement, the Resurrection and the Symbols of Islām and then have *kufr* and *shirk* applied to him? Also bearing in mind that they are not pleased with being called *Mushrikeen* and rather virulently flee from the term?"

The answer to this could be: A Muslim may fall into corrupt beliefs such as believing in the stars or believing that the creation can bring harm or benefit, or a Muslim may fall into acts such as prostrating to other than Allāh and other practices. These actions, and those like them, remove the name of Islām from a person and render the *shirk* and *kufr* to be applied to the person at which point the person will become a *Mushrik* and a *Murtad*

Tāreekh al-Kabeer. All are narrated via a man from Bani Kāhil from Abū Mūsā al-'Ash'arī, al-Haythamī said in *al-Majma'*, vol.10, p.223: "Narrated by Ahmad and at-Tabarānī in *al-Kabeer* and *al-Awsat* and the narrators of Ahmad are sound except for Abū 'Alī and Wathaq ibn Hibbān." Also reported by Abū Ya'la in his *Musnad* (vol.1, p.60-2, *hadeeth* no.54, 55, 56) from the *hadeeth* of Hudhayfah from Abū Bakr in a *marfū'* form and from the *hadeeth* of Mu'qal bin Yasār in *marfū'* form, mentioned by al-Hāfidh in *al-Matālib* (vol.3, p.183) and referred it to the *Musnad* of Ishāq ibn Rāhawayh and Abū Bakr al-Marwazī narrated it in *Musnad* Abū Bakr (p.55); Bukhārī in *Adab al-Mufrad* (p.105) from the narration of Mu'qal from Abū Bakr in *marfū'* form, related by at-Tirmidhī (p.397). al-Haythamī said in *al-Majma'* (vol.10, p.224): "Related by Abū Ya'la from his Shaykh 'Umar bin al-Husayn al-'Aqlī, who is *matrook*). Al-Albānī said in *Saheeh al-Jāmi'* (vol.1, p.694, *hadeeth* no.3731) that it is *saheeh*. Abū Nu'aym also relayed it in *al-Hilyah* (vol.7, p.112) from the *hadeeth* Qays bin Hāzim from Abū Bakr and al-Albānī declared it *saheeh* in *Saheeh al-Jāmi'*, vol.1, p.693, *hadeeth* no.3730

(apostate). If this is not the case, then why did the companions deem those who rejected *Zakāh* as being disbelievers, fight against them and reach agreement on their apostasy? What is the meaning of apostasy? What is the meaning of the statement of the Prophet ﷺ: *"The blood of a Muslim person is not permitted (to shed) except in three cases: leaving his Deen..."[1]* And he ﷺ also said *"Whoever changes his religion – kill him (i.e. execute)."[2]*

So how can it be said after this that a Muslim could never ever fall into *shirk* and that the one who is described with Islām cannot possibly fall into *kufr* and *shirk* which expels him from Islām? So the intent is not to say that *kufr* and *shirk* cannot be applied to a specific Muslim but rather that this can only be applied after the texts have been explained to him and the proofs are established on him. Yet if there are no proofs to establish and then the person continues being stubborn and rejecting the proofs out of pride then there is no doubt that major *shirk* can rightfully be applied to the

---

[1] Reported by al-Bukhārī, vol.8, p.38, *Kitāb ud-Dīyāt* [Book of Blood-Monies]; Muslim, vol.3, p.1303, hadeeth no.1686.

[2] Reported by al-Bukhārī, vol.8, p.50, *Kitāb Istitābat ul-MurtaDeen*.

[TN]: This hadeeth is not to be implemented or carried out by the average Muslim who reads it! rather, it is for the head of state to implement such a regulation. When we discuss apostasy and its punishment in Islamic law, tradition and scholarship we in no way suggest that the common Muslim has the right to implement its punishment whenever he feels like within a non-Muslim country, or for vigilante Muslim groups to search out those who commit this crime in order to enact the punishment within a non-Muslim or Muslim country.

person. No one should think that we are being hasty in pronouncing *takfeer* of the people who are monotheists and applying *shirk* to them as the terms *shirk* and *kufr* are both mentioned within the Divine Legislation and they are not to be applied except with Divinely Legislated principles. So just as it is not permissible to make *takfeer* of a Muslim without right likewise it is not permissible to refrain from making *takfeer* of an actual Mushrik or of one who has really left the Islām.

It is found within the *Salaf* that they made *takfeer* of specific people who rightfully deserved it and applied *kufr* and *shirk* to them. if not can one imagine that we refrain from applying *kufr* to the one who says *"I pronounce the Shahādatayn, I pray, fast, give Zakāh and make Hajj, but I say that Ahmad al-Qādiyānī is a Messenger from Allāh"* and *"I say that the spirit of God is in the body of Sayyid Badawī"?* The truth is more glorified and worthy than anyone, so the accusation of making *takfeer* should not be used as a brandished sword over the necks of the people of truth to prevent them from applying the term of *kufr* to those who deserve it, along with maintaining the Divinely Legislated principles such as knowledge of the one who done the action and exhausting the preventative factors such as compulsion for example. *Al-'Allāmah* al-Alūsī al-Hanafi has some important words in regards to takfeer of the grave-worshippers and his words support the verifications of *Shaykh ul-Islām* Ibn Taymiyyah G regarding not being hasty in making *takfeer* except after the proofs have been established and the way has been made apparent (to the person). Al-Alūsī G said:

> None of the people of knowledge, who are referred to, ceased deeming the grave-worshippers as being upon *kufr*. Yet they always stated that the person is not to be executed until he repents and the person is not to be judged as having *kufr* until the proofs have been established on the person and the likes of such statements can be found from the people of knowledge. *Shaykh ul-Islām* Ibn Taymiyyah has some other texts which we will transmit fully for further benefit.[1]

Then al-Alūsī transmitted a number of texts from *Shaykh ul-Islām* Ibn Taymiyyah in affirming this issue. Abū Ghuddah al-Hanafī also has an important piece of research on refraining from being hasty in takfeer and that *takfeer* should not be done except after the proofs have been established on the one who commits *kufr* and *shirk*. Abū Ghuddah supports his statements with verifications from *Shaykh ul-Islām* Ibn Taymiyyah and others from the people of knowledge from the Hanafī scholars and others. The conclusion from Abū Ghuddah's words is that *takfeer* of the people of innovation is not permissible unless they have committed open *kufr* or clear *shirk* and have denied something which is known by the *Deen* by necessity, and after the proofs have been established on them and the way has been

---

[1] See *Ghāyat ul-Amānī*, vol.1, pp.30-31

made clear to them. Only after this can one be judged as being upon *kufr*, apostasized and left the religion of Islām.[1]

Shaykh ul-Islām Ibn Taymiyyah ﷺ said:

The basis of that is a statement which is kufr in the Book, Sunnah and ijmā' is deemed as kufr based on what the evidences from the *Sharee'ah* indicate. Īmān in the regulations that have arrived from Allāh and His messenger are not like what is used to judge people in accordance with their minds and desires. It is not obligatory to judge with *kufr* every person who says something of *kufr* until the proofs have been established on him and the conditions of *takfeer* have been applied along with the preventative factors. So for example if someone says that alcohol or interest is *halāl* due to the person just having come into the fold of Islām or due to living far away in the remote regions; or he heard some words that he did not believe was from the Noble Qur'ān or from the ahādeeth of the Messenger of Allāh ﷺ, just like some of the Salaf denied things until they were verified as having been said by the Prophet ﷺ.

Then *Shaykh ul-Islām* Ibn Taymiyyah said:

So those are not to be made *takfeer* upon until the proofs of the Message have been established upon them, as Allāh says,

---

[1] See *at-Tatimmat ul-Khāsah min Tatimmāt* of Abū Ghuddah to the end of the book *al-Muqidhah* by adh-Dhahabī, pp.146-165.

﴿لِئَلاَّ يَكُونَ لِلنَّاسِ عَلَى اللّهِ حُجَّةٌ بَعْدَ الرُّسُلِ﴾

"...so that mankind will have no argument against Allāh after the Messengers." *{an-Nisā (4): 165}*

Allāh forgave this Ummah for its errors and forgetfulness.[1]

Shaykh ul-Islām Ibn Taymiyyah ﷺ said:

As for takfeer then it is correct that whoever from the Ummah of Muhammad ﷺ strives *(ijtahada)* to know the truth and then errs then *kufr* is not to be applied to the person, rather the person is forgiven for his error. Whoever is shown clearly what the Messenger came with and then opposes the Messenger after the guidance has been shown to them, and follows a way other than the way of the believers – is a disbeliever. Whoever follows his desires and falls short seeking the truth and speaks without knowledge is disobedient and sinful and the person can be a sinner or have good deeds which outweigh his bad deeds.[2]

Ibn Taymiyyah stated in another instance:

This is with the fact that I have always (forbade), and those who sit with me know this from me, that I am of those who forbid ascribing *takfeer, tasfeeq* and disobedience to a specific person until it is known

---

[1] *Majmū' al-Fatāwā*, vol.35, p.165

[2] *Majmū l-Fatāwā*, vol.12, p.180

that the Prophetic proof has been established on the person. Such a proof is of the level which if a person were to deny would be a disbeliever, or a *fāsiq* (sinner) or disobedient at other times. I affirm that Allāh has forgiven the mistakes of this Ummah and this covers both matters of reports of sayings and knowledge-related issues. The Salaf used to discuss many issues and they did not testify that a specific person with kufr, fisq or disobedience.[1]

Then he mentioned examples of this and said:

I explained that what has been transmitted from the Salaf and the Imāms in regards to attaching *takfeer* to one who had said such and such a statement is also correct, however there has to be a distinction between applying it and specifying it.

Then Ibn Taymiyyah said:

Takfeer is a form of threat so it can be made on one who denies something said by the Messenger 攤, however the person may be new in Islām or may have been raised in the remote regions – and these types of people are not made *takfeer* of for rejection until the proofs have been established on them. It may also be the case that the man has not heard certain texts or has heard them but does not fully ascertain them or turns away from them, this has to be fully

---

[1] Ibid., vol.3, p.229

interpreted as he maybe mistaken. I used to always mention the hadeeth which is in the Two Saheehs about the man who said: *""When I have died, burn me, then crush me and scatter [my ashes] into the sea, for, by Allah, if my Lord takes me, He will punish me in a manner in which He has not punished anybody else." So the people did that to him. Then Allāh said to the earth: Produce what you have taken- and there he was! And Allāh said to the man: "What induced you to do what you did?" The man said: "I was in fear of You, O my Lord." Because of that Allāh forgave him. "*[1] So this man doubted the Power of Allāh and bringing him back to life and actually believed that he would not be resurrected and this in itself is *kufr* by the agreement of the Muslims. However, the man was ignorant and did not know that that was *kufr* so he was still a believer who as he had fear that Allāh would punish him, yet Allāh forgave him on account of that. The one who makes an incorrect interpretation who is from the people of *ijtihād* safeguards following the Messenger of Allāh 鸒 and is therefore more fitting to receive forgiveness than the other person (i.e. who is ignorant).[2]

Imām Muhammad bin Sālih al-'Uthaymeen 鸒 said:

---

[1] Reported by al-Bukhārī, vol.4, pp.144, 151, *Kitāb ul-Anbiyā*; Muslim, vol.4, p.2110, *hadeeth* no. 2756.

[2] *Majmū' al-Fatāwā*, vol.3, p.229

So if someone says "do you make *takfeer* and *tasfeeq* of those who make incorrect interpretations?" We say: the ruling of *takfeer* and *tasfeeq* is not our right rather it is the right of Allāh and His Messenger 攤, it is from the Divine Legislated regulations (*Ahkām ush-Shar'iyyah*) which are based on the Book and the Sunnah. So there has to be the utmost verification so that none is branded with *kufr* or *fisq* except based on what the Book and Sunnah judge is a person's *kufr* or *fisq*. The basis of a Muslim is apparently that he is trustworthy and that his Islam remains as does his trustworthiness until this has been removed from him based on Shari' proof. It is not permissible to be easy in making *takfeer* or *tasfeeq* of a Muslim because this involved two significant prohibited matters:

Firstly: Lying on Allāh in terms of ruling and the one being ruled upon and judged.

Secondly: Falling into abusing and falsely accusing his Muslim brother if he is not as is claimed. In Saheeh Muslim[1] it is reported from 'Abdullāh bin 'Umar 攤 that the Prophet 攤 said: *"If a man deems his brother has having kufr then the ruling will apply to one of them."*[2] In another narration it says, *"Either the man is as how his*

---

[1] *Kitāb ul-Īmān, 'Bāb Bayān Hāl man Qāla li Akheehi Muslim: "Yā Kāfir"'* [Chapter: An Explanation of the Condition of the One who Says to his Muslim Brother: "*O you disbeliever*"], vol.1, p.79, hadeeth no.111

[2] Reported by Muslim, vol.1, p.79, hadeeth no.60

brother said or it will return back to the one who says it (i.e. that someone is a disbeliever)."[1] Also from Abū Dharr ❀ from the Prophet ❀ who said: "*Whoever claims that a man has kufr or says that the man is an enemy of Allāh and yet is no like that then it will return upon the claimant.*"[2]

So based on this before a Muslim can be judged as having *kufr* or *fisq* two matters have to be looked at:

Firstly: The evidences from the Book and the Sunnah upon that particular saying or action which have necessitated *kufr* or *fisq* to be applied to the person.

Secondly: The applicability of the ruling upon the specific one who made the statement or did the specific action so that the conditions of *takfeer* or *tasfeeq* can be fully exhausted in regards to the person and after the preventative factors have also been exhausted. From the most important conditions are that the person had full knowledge of his opposition (to Islām) which necessitated him becoming a disbeliever or a *fāsiq* (sinner), this is based on the saying of Allāh,

---

[1] *Kitāb ul-Īmān, 'Bāb Bayān Hāl man Qāla li Akheehi Muslim: "Yā Kāfir"'* [Chapter: An Explanation of the Condition of the One who Says to his Muslim Brother: "*O you disbeliever*"], vol.1, p.79

[2] Reported by Muslim in *Kitāb ul-Īmān, Bāb Bayān Hāl man Qāla li Akheehi Muslim: "Yā Kāfir"'* [Chapter: An Explanation of the Condition of the One who Says to his Muslim Brother: "*O you disbeliever*"], vol.1, p.79, hadeeth no.112.

﴿وَمَن يُشَاقِقِ ٱلرَّسُولَ مِنۢ بَعْدِ مَا تَبَيَّنَ لَهُ ٱلْهُدَىٰ وَيَتَّبِعْ غَيْرَ سَبِيلِ ٱلْمُؤْمِنِينَ نُوَلِّهِۦ مَا تَوَلَّىٰ وَنُصْلِهِۦ جَهَنَّمَ ۖ وَسَآءَتْ مَصِيرًا ﴾

"And whoever opposes the Messenger after guidance has become clear to him and follows other than the way of the believers We will give him what he has taken and drive him into Hell, and evil it is as a destination." *{an-Nisā (4): 115}*

And Allāh says,

﴿وَمَا كَانَ اللَّهُ لِيُضِلَّ قَوْماً بَعْدَ إِذْ هَدَاهُمْ حَتَّى يُبَيِّنَ لَهُم مَّا يَتَّقُونَ إِنَّ اللَّهَ بِكُلِّ شَيْءٍ عَلِيمٌ – إِنَّ اللَّهَ لَهُ مُلْكُ السَّمَـٰوَتِ وَالْأَرْضِ يُحْىٖ وَيُمِيتُ وَمَا لَكُم مِّن دُونِ اللَّهِ مِن وَلِىٍّ وَلاَ نَصِيرٍ ﴾

"And Allāh will never lead a people astray after He has guided them until He makes clear to them what they should avoid. Indeed, to Allāh belongs the dominion of the heavens and the earth; He gives life and causes death. And you have not besides Allāh any protector or any helper." *{at-Tawbah (9): 115-116}*

For this reason the people of knowledge said: the one who denies the obligations is not made takfeer of if he is new in Islām until it is made clear to him. From the preventative factors which do not necessitate applying *kufr* or *fisq* to a person are: if a person was compelled to do something without being pleased with that, in this case such a person is not made *takfeer* of. This is based on when Allāh says,

﴿مَن كَفَرَ بِاللَّهِ مِن بَعْدِ إِيمَـٰنِهِ إِلَّا مَنْ أُكْرِهَ وَقَلْبُهُ مُطْمَئِنٌّ بِالْإِيمَـٰنِ وَلَـٰكِن مَّن شَرَحَ بِالْكُفْرِ صَدْرًا فَعَلَيْهِمْ غَضَبٌ مِّنَ اللَّهِ وَلَهُمْ عَذَابٌ عَظِيمٌ﴾

"Whoever disbelieves in Allāh after his belief, except for one who is forced [to renounce his religion] while his heart is secure in faith. But those who [willingly] open their breasts to disbelief, upon them is wrath from Allāh, and for them is a great punishment..." *{an-Nahl (16): 106}*

Also from the preventative factors is: when a person is not thinking straight and does not know what he is saying out of intense joy, grief, fear or the like. The evidence for this is what has been reported in Saheeh Muslim from Anas bin Mālik ﷺ who said: the Messenger of Allāh ﷺ said: *"Allah is more pleased with the repentance of His believing servant than a person who loses his riding beast carrying food and drink. Having lost all hope he lies down in the shade disappointed about his camel and then after a while he gets up to find the camel standing before him. He takes hold of his nose string and then out of boundless joy says:*

'O Allāh! You are my servant and I am Your Lord!' He commits this mistake out of extreme delight. "[1]

From this then, the statements of the people of knowledge and their Divinely Legislated principles in regards to the issue of *takfeer* become clear to us, and Allāh knows best.

---

[1] *Al-Qawā'id ul-Muthlā fi's-Sifātillāh al-Husnā*, pp.116-119, the hadeeth is reported al-Bukhārī, vol.7, p147, *Kitāb ud-Da'wāt*; Muslim, vol.4, p.2104, hadeeth no.2747.

⊰ Conclusion ⊱

This research has discovered a number of results, the most important of which are:

Firstly: The Hanafi *'Ulama* have a praiseworthy role in refuting the people of *bida'* (innovation) from the grave-worshippers and explaining *shirk* along with its types, means and manifestations within Islamic societies.

Secondly: Many Muslims are ignorant of the reality of *tawheed* and for that reason fell into different types of *shirk* from whence they did not perceive.

Thirdly: The understanding of *shirk* with some Muslims is that it just means worshipping stones, trees and idols and for that reason they themselves began to associate partners with Allāh in obedience, *inqiyād* (compliance), *mahabbah* (love) and worship and this occurred to them due to their ignorance of the reality of servitude and *shirk*.

Fourthly: *shirk* in all of its facets and manifestations is nothing but a test for the people and a humiliation, as they submissively dedicate themselves to the creation and have servitude to personalities who themselves are unable to possess the ability to harm or benefit, or to bring death, give life or resurrect.

Fifthly: The Divine Legislation has put in place significant precautions and the most important of these precautions are to prevent every saying, action or intent that is *shirk* or a means to *shirk*.

Finally, this small effort is bound to have discrepancies and shortcomings because shortcomings and errors are from the attributes from the creation, so I hope that the respected reader will excuse me for all shortcomings and discrepancies.

I ask Allāh for this work to be sincerely for His Noble Countenance and to grant us all success to the guidance of His Book and to follow the Sunnah of His Messenger, our Prophet Muhammad ﷺ.

Sufficient is Allāh for us and He is the Best disposer of affairs and our final du'ā is all praise is due to Allāh the Lord of the Worlds.

Shirk According To Scholars From

The Shāfi'ī Madhhab

⊰ Introduction ⊱

Tawheed has a great effect in the lives of people and within the society and its fruits have the most beautiful effects such as:

Expelling a person from servitude to other than Allāh, as *tawheed* involves a person worshipping only his Creator, Mighty and Majestic, whereas *shirk* involves a person worshipping a creation which is like him and neither possesses harm nor benefit, neither the ability to give death nor life. *Tawheed* frees a person's mind from superstition, frees his conscious from humbleness and servility and frees his life from being overcome by transgressors. This is what the Mushrikeen knew from the meaning of *La ilaha il-Allāh* so they set up enmity against the Messengers and fought against them.

Controlling Manners and working to adorn them, because a Muslim moves with every action and moment of his life in order to please Allāh in all states. Allāh says,

$$﴿ ضَرَبَ اللَّهُ مَثَلًا رَّجُلًا فِيهِ شُرَكَاءُ مُتَشَاكِسُونَ وَرَجُلًا سَلَمًا لِّرَجُلٍ هَلْ يَسْتَوِيَانِ مَثَلًا ﴾$$

"Allāh presents an example: a slave owned by quarreling partners and another belonging exclusively to one man are they equal in comparison?" *{az-Zumar (39): 29}*

The first example is like one who worships multiple gods trying to please all of them and the second example is the one who only worships the One True God.

The soul finding strong faith, Allāh says,

﴿وَكَيْفَ أَخَافُ مَا أَشْرَكْتُمْ وَلاَ تَخَافُونَ أَنَّكُمْ أَشْرَكْتُم بِاللّهِ مَا لَمْ يُنَزِّلْ بِهِ عَلَيْكُمْ سُلْطَانًا فَأَيُّ الْفَرِيقَيْنِ أَحَقُّ بِالأَمْنِ إِن كُنتُمْ تَعْلَمُونَ الَّذِينَ آمَنُواْ وَلَمْ يَلْبِسُواْ إِيمَانَهُم بِظُلْمٍ أُوْلَـئِكَ لَهُمُ الأَمْنُ وَهُم مُّهْتَدُونَ﴾

"And how should I fear what you associate while you do not fear that you have associated with Allāh that for which He has not sent down to you any authority? So which of the two parties has more right to security, if you should know? They who believe and do not mix their belief with injustice - those will have security, and they are [rightly] guided."

{al-An'ām (6): 81-2}

The believer always has trust in Allāh, turning to Him knowing that He possesses the Dominion, this leads to the believer having faith and trust in Allāh within his self, trusting Him and being assured of Him. How could this not be the case when He sees humans do not posses anything and rather it is only Allāh who possesses the dominion, look at the statement of Nūh ﷺ,

﴿وَاتْلُ عَلَيْهِمْ نَبَأَ نُوحٍ إِذْ قَالَ لِقَوْمِهِ يَا قَوْمِ إِن كَانَ كَبُرَ عَلَيْكُم مَّقَامِي وَتَذْكِيرِي بِآيَاتِ اللَّهِ فَعَلَى اللَّهِ تَوَكَّلْتُ فَأَجْمِعُواْ أَمْرَكُمْ وَشُرَكَاءكُمْ ثُمَّ لاَ يَكُنْ أَمْرُكُمْ عَلَيْكُمْ غُمَّةً ثُمَّ اقْضُواْ إِلَيَّ وَلاَ تُنظِرُونِ﴾

"And recite to them the news of Noah, when he said to his people, "O my people, if my residence and my reminding of the signs of Allāh has become burdensome upon you then I have relied upon Allāh. So resolve upon your plan and [call upon] your associates. Then let not your plan be obscure to you. Then carry it out upon me and do not give me respite."

{Yūnus (10): 71}

And Hūd ﷺ said to his people,

﴿مِن دُونِهِ فَكِيدُونِي جَمِيعًا ثُمَّ لاَ تُنظِرُونِ إِنِّي تَوَكَّلْتُ عَلَى اللَّهِ رَبِّي وَرَبِّكُم مَّا مِن دَآبَّةٍ إِلاَّ هُوَ آخِذٌ بِنَاصِيَتِهَا إِنَّ رَبِّي عَلَى صِرَاطٍ مُّسْتَقِيمٍ﴾

"['I call Allāh to witness and bear you witness that I am free from that which you ascribe as partners in worship,] other than Him. So plot against me all together; then do not give me respite. Indeed, I have relied upon Allāh, my Lord and your Lord. There

123

is no creature but that He holds its forelock. Indeed, my Lord is on a path [that is] straight.'" *{Hūd (11): 55-56}*

These souls have attained trust, assurance and faith in Allāh due to their comprehension of the Ability of Allāh and His Glory. These souls have also realised the feebleness of creation and that creation does not have a share of this whatsoever.

Laying down the basis of brotherhood and equality: Islām is a religion of *tawheed*, it makes all people the same in humility to their Lord ﷻ. They are not to take lords from among them to be worshipped other than Allāh and they are not to enslave each other, rather all people are equal in humanity. All *Muwahhiddūn* are equal in terms of the rights and obligations they have to perform and there is no virtue of any of them over another except in *taqwa* and righteous actions. Therefore, there is neither discrimination in terms of colour or race nor in occupation or anything else, Allāh says,

$$﴿إِنَّ أَكْرَمَكُمْ عِندَ اللَّهِ أَتْقَاكُمْ﴾$$

"Indeed, the most noble of you in the sight of Allāh is the most righteous of you." *{al-Hujurāt (49): 13}*

◄ The Harms and Corruptions of Shirk ►

Contrary to the positive effects and fruits of *tawheed* are the corruptions and harms of shirk which include:

Humiliation, Via worshipping other than Allāh and worshipping the creation like him which neither benefits nor harms yet is taken as an object of worship and homage even though it is created like the person worshipping it. Indeed, at times a person will even worship that which is lower than him! Like a cow, tree, stone or the likes. So is it befitting for an intelligent and noble person to be like this and is there anything more humiliating than this?!

Being superstitious, this is because a person believes something from the creation can benefit or harm and thus makes up superstitions and legends surrounding it all of which do not agree with one's intellect.

Shirk is the worst oppression, Allāh says,

﴿وَالْكَافِرُونَ هُمُ الظَّالِمُونَ﴾

"And the disbelievers they are the wrongdoers." *{Baqara (2): 254}*

And Allāh says,

﴿إِنَّ الشِّرْكَ لَظُلْمٌ عَظِيمٌ﴾

"Indeed, association [with Him] is great injustice." *{Luqmān (31): 13}*

What oppression is worse than after Allāh having created you and provided for you, you then go and worship and thank other than Him?

Shirk causes fear and paranoia, this is because *mushrik* does not trust in Allāh and is entrenched in delusions and superstitions and is thus afraid of everything. The *mushrik* fears for his life, his sustenance and everything in life!

Negative effects in human life, *Shirk* causes a person to depend on others for his intercession just as how the Christian depends on the Messiah ﷺ.

Entry into the Hell-Fire, *shirk* is one of the main reasons which lead to entry into the Hellfire, Allāh says,

﴿ إِنَّهُ مَن يُشْرِكْ بِاللَّهِ فَقَدْ حَرَّمَ اللَّهُ عَلَيْهِ الْجَنَّةَ وَمَأْوَاهُ النَّارُ وَمَا لِلظَّالِمِينَ مِنْ أَنصَارٍ ﴾

"Indeed, he who associates others with Allāh, Allāh has forbidden him Paradise, and his refuge is the Fire. And there are not for the wrongdoers any helpers." *{al-Mā'idah (5): 72}*

Tawheed is from the main reasons for entry into Paradise while the *mushrik* has no destination except for the Hellfire because his sin (of *shirk*) will not be forgiven at all, Allāh says,

126

﴿إِنَّ اللّهَ لاَ يَغْفِرُ أَن يُشْرَكَ بِهِ وَيَغْفِرُ مَا دُونَ ذَلِكَ لِمَن يَشَاءُ وَمَن يُشْرِكْ بِاللّهِ فَقَدِ افْتَرَى إِثْمًا عَظِيمًا﴾

"Indeed, Allāh does not forgive association with Him..."

{an-Nisā (4): 48}

These are some of the corruptions of *shirk* and its harmful effects on the human soul within this life and the next. What is well known is that *shirk* is the main thing that the Qurʾān warns against and its proofs and verses invalidate *shirk*. The Qurʾān also cursed the one who does actions of *shirk* and judges the one who does it with Hellfire. The Qurʾān mentions that there are many corruptions for humans linked to *shirk* and thus warned against it. For this reason I wanted to explain the efforts of the Shāfiʿī scholars in explaining *shirk*, its means, types and the like based upon what I have come across from their books.

The Shāfiʿiyyah: They ascribe themselves in branches of *fiqh* to the great Imām, the ocean, the mountain of knowledge, the Mujaddid of his era at the beginning of 200 AH,[1] one of the four Imams of the Muslims that are followed in subsidiary matters of *fiqh*. Imām ash-Shāfiʿī was born in 150 AH and died in 204 AH. His *madhhab* became widespread in al-ʾIrāq, Shām, Egypt, the Hijāz, Yemen and elsewhere. His *madhhab* is still the

---

[1] *Taqreeb ut-Tahdheeb*, vol.2, p.142, no.31

official *madhhab* in some Islamic countries today, may Allāh have mercy on him and reward him.

I ask Allāh to bring benefit to all of the Muslims with this book and place it in our scales on the Day of Judgement. Sufficient is Allāh for us and He is the Best Guardian, and our final duā' is all praise is due to Allāh, the Lord of the Worlds.

⊰ Definition of Shirk According to the Shāfiʿī Scholars ⊱

Al-Azhari ash-Shāfiʿī said:

Allāh says, while informing of his worshipper Luqmān the wise that he said to his son,

$$﴿لَا تُشْرِكْ بِاللَّهِ إِنَّ الشِّرْكَ لَظُلْمٌ عَظِيمٌ﴾$$

"Do not associate partners with Allāh. Indeed, association [with Him] is great injustice." *{Luqmān (31): 13}*

Shirk is that you associate a partner with Allāh in His Rubūbiyyah and there is a 'bā' (i.e. 'with')…

$$﴿لَا تُشْرِكْ بِاللَّهِ﴾$$

"Do not associate partners with Allāh"

…because the verse means that nothing can be compared with Him and so do not ascribe a partner to Him, likewise Allāh says,

$$﴿بِمَا أَشْرَكُوا بِاللَّهِ مَا لَمْ يُنَزِّلْ بِهِ سُلْطَانًا﴾$$

"…for what they have associated with Allāh of which He had not sent down [any] authority." *{Āli ʾImrān (3): 151}*

129

This means to make something equal with Him and whoever makes Allāh equal with something from the creation has become a Mushik because Allāh has no partners, no associate and no helper.[1]

Ar-Rāghib al-Asbahānī said:

Greater *shirk* is to affirm for Allāh a partner, so it is said that "a person associated a partner with Allāh" and this is the worst type of *kufr*.[2]

Al-Munāwī stated:

Shirk: applying the affair of The One to one who has not portion of the matter.[3]

Allāmah 'Ali Suwaydī ash-Shāfi'ī[4] said in his explanation of *shirk* and his warning against its danger:

---

[1] *Tahdheeb ul-Lughah*, vol.10, p.16

[2] *Al-Muwatta*, p.452

[3] *At-Tawaqquf 'alā Mihāt it-Ta'arruf*, p.428

[4] [TN]: He is 'Ali bin Muhammad bin Sa'eed as-Suwaydī al-Baghdādī al-Abbāsi who was a scholar of *hadeeth* and history. Born in Baghdad, he died in Damascus in 1232 AH, he had a number of writings and corresponded with Imam Muhammad ibn 'AbdulWahhāb. As-Suwaydī tried to convince the governor of Baghdad, Sulayman Pasha as-Sagheer, to adhere to the *da'wah* of Imam Muhammad ibn 'AbdulWahhāb and his methodology was the same as Muhammad ibn 'AbdulWahhāb's and as-Suwaydī instilled within his student ShihābudDeen al-Alūsī (1802-1854 CE) with many of the ideas and teachings of Imam Muhammad ibn 'AbdulWahhāb. From this point on the Alūsī family of scholars began defending Imām Muhammad ibn'AbdulWahhāb.

You should know- may Allāh protect me and you from *shirk*, *kufr* and misguidance and grant us success to those words and actions that He loves and is pleased with – that *shirk* opposes *tawheed* and that both of them cannot be combined just as *kufr* opposes *īmān* due to them both being mutually contradictory. So if it is said *"this person is a Muwahhid"* then this means that he believes in the Oneness of Allāh without partner. A person is not a *Muwahhid* with the sought-after *tawheed* unless he has freed himself from all that which includes *shirk*.

Contrary to the *Muwahhid* is the *Mushrik* who has *shirk* in certain types whether in: statements, conditions, actions or in beliefs, dealings or in his agreement and beautifying of it or his being pleased in speaking with it and listening to it. During *Jāhilyyah* the polytheists associated in their worship what their corrupted minds had beautified and this blind following of this clear misguidance led them to become devoted to the worship of idols, trees, statues and graves seeking blessings from them, hoping for their intercession and turning to them. Many misguided arts have become popularised from this filthy *shirk* and void branches were introduced from this such as the ignorant beliefs in omens, vows to idols, incantations magic spells and the use of amulets. As a result, they associated between the Creator and the creation in love, hope, fear, withholding, giving, closeness and farness. The people remained

131

steeped in this misguidance until they had conjured up their own religion that Allāh had not ordained. They also remained in this utter ignorance and blind opposition until Allāh sent His Prophet *al-Mustapha* (lit. the chosen one, i.e. Muhammad ﷺ) as a bringer of glad tidings, a warner and a caller to Allāh with His Light. For that reason you see that the Qur'ān and the *hadeeth* mention *shirk* and the *Mushrikeen* more than it mentions *kufr* and the *Kāfireen*...[1]

After this explanation, we bring attention to the fact that *shirk* in *Ulūhiyyah* was not mentioned (by the scholar above) even though *Tawheed Ulūhiyyah* is the basis of the *Deen* of Islām and was what caused the disagreement between the Messengers and their people and was what all the Messengers were sent for. As Allāh said,

﴿وَمَا أَرْسَلْنَا مِن قَبْلِكَ مِن رَّسُولٍ إِلَّا نُوحِي إِلَيْهِ أَنَّهُ لَا إِلَهَ إِلَّا أَنَا فَاعْبُدُونِ﴾

"And We sent not before you any messenger except that We revealed to him that there is no deity except Me, so worship Me." *{al-Anbiyā (21): 25}*

---

[1] *Al-'Iqd uth-Thameen*, pp.18-19

⚜ An Explanation of the Types of Shirk According to Some of the Shāfiʿī Scholars ⚜

Ar-Rāghib al-Asbahānī said:

The *shirk* that people commit in the religion are of two types: greater *shirk* which affirms a partner for Allāh, this is the greatest *kufr* and secondly: hidden *shirk* and *nifāq* (hipocracy).[1]

Allāmah ʾAli Suwaydī ash-Shāfiʾī:

You should know that *shirk* can either be in *Rubūbiyyah* or in *Ulūhiyyah*. Secondly, it can either be in belief or in dealings with the Lord. This second type branches off into *Shirk-ul-Ībādah* which splits up into statements and actions and within both is major *shirk* which is unforgivable. As for minor *shirk,* then that can be forgiven yet our speech now is regarding major *shirk* which Allāh has obligated us to be free from. The *tawheed* of the worshipper is not perfected until after he has understood *shirk*, its types and causes, just as the Poet said,

I knew the evil so as not to fall into it,

Whoever does not know the good from the evil will fall into it.

---

[1] *Al-Mufradāt*, p.452

133

In order to warn from this danger, the Messenger of Allāh ﷺ sought refuge from it because he knew the most from the people and had the utmost fear of Allāh as is relayed from him when he said ﷺ *"O Allāh I seek refuge in you from associating anything in worship with you while I know and I seek refuge in you from associating anything in worship with you while I do not know."* There are other *du'ā* that he mentioned. The Khaleel of Allāh Ibrāheem ﷺ, when he said,

$$﴿وَاجْنُبْنِي وَبَنِيَّ أَن نَّعْبُدَ الأَصْنَامَ﴾$$

"...and keep me and my sons away from worshipping idols."

{Ibrāheem (14): 35}

Although his children were Prophets and Messengers! So if this was the last of the Prophets and this was how the Friend of the Lord of the Worlds was, that they both sought refuge from shirk and sought liberation with Allāh from and they both feared falling into it and they were the best of the Messengers, so what about others whoever they may be!?

Shirk in *Rubūbiyyah*: this was not stated by any of the *kuffār* and no one has stated that there is another creator in existence. Even if there has arisen *ta'teel* from some of the *kuffār* in terms of *Rubūbiyyah*, such as the *ta'teel* of Pharaoh and his people. As for *shirk* in *Ulūhiyyah*, then no one says that the two worlds have separate gods that are the same except for the deists. As for the idolators who worship, then they do not say that there are a multiplicity of creators, even if they apply divinity to the gods that they worship.[1]

He also said in another instance:

In conclusion, *shirk* is of two types: *shirk* in *Rubūbiyyah* wherein another god is set up as a Creator other than Allāh and *shirk* in *Ulūhiyyah* is wherein other than Allāh is called upon by *du'ā'*.[2]

Ahmad bin Hajar Āl Būtāmī ash-Shāfi'ī said, in affirming the speech of Shaykh ul-Islām Ibn Taymiyyah:

Shirk is of two types: major and minor and whoever is free from them both will enter Paradise and whoever dies upon major *shirk* will enter the Hellfire. Whoever is free from major *shirk* yet commits some aspects of minor *shirk* and has some good deeds which outweigh, that person will enter Paradise. Whoever is free from major *shirk* yet has committed much in the way of minor *shirk* to the extent that his evil actions outweigh, then such a person will enter

---

[1] *Al-'Iqd uth-Thameen fī Bayān Masā'il id-Deen*, pp.119-120

[2] Ibid., p.123. From the proofs that *du'ā* to other than Allāh is *shirk* is the saying of Allāh, **"And your Lord says, "Call upon Me; I will respond to you." Indeed, those who disdain My worship will enter Hell [rendered] contemptible."** {*Ghāfir (40): 60*} And His saying: **"And I will leave you and those you invoke other than Allāh and will invoke my Lord. I expect that I will not be in invocation to my Lord unhappy." So when he had left them and those they worshipped other than Allāh, We gave him Isāc and Jacob..."** {*Maryam (19): 48-9*} So *duā'* is an act of worship and directing this act of worship to other than Allāh is to associate a partner with Allāh.

Hellfire. *Shirk* will be take a person to Hell if the majority of it has been committed or if much minor *shirk* has been committed. However, if the minor *shirk* is little and the culprit has much sincerity then this will not render a person as being adequate for Hell. Major *shirk* is: *sujūd* (prostration),[1] vows to other than Allāh.[2] Minor *shirk* is: *riyā* (showing off)[3] and making oaths to other than Allāh[4] if the person did not intend glorification of the creation in a manner which only Allāh should be glorified.[5]

---

[1] The proof that *sujūd* to other than Allāh is *shirk* is the saying of Allāh, **"So exalt [Allāh] with praise of your Lord and be of those who prostrate [to Him]. And worship your Lord until there comes to you the certainty (death)."** *{Al-Hijr (15): 98-9}* And the Prophet ﷺ said: *"If I were to instruct anyone to prostrate to another other than Allāh then I would instructed the wife to prostrate to her husband."*

[2] The proof about making vows is the saying of Allāh, **"Then let them end their untidiness and fulfil their vows and perform tawāf around the ancient House."** *{al-Hajj (22): 29}* And Allāh says, **"They [are those who] fulfill [their] vows…"** *{al-Insān (76): 7}*

[3] Based on Allāh's saying, **"…showing [themselves to] the people and not remembering Allāh except a little…"** *{an-Nisā (4): 142}*

[4] Based on the saying of the Messenger ﷺ *"Whoever swears an oath to other than Allāh has committed shirk."*

[5] *Tatheer ul-Janān wa'l-Arkān 'an Darn ish-Shirk wa'l-Kufrān*, pp.38-9.

﷽ The Means to Shirk That the Shāfi'ī Scholars Cautioned Against in Order to Preserve Tawheed ﷽

It has been transmitted from Imam ash-Shāfi'ī and his followers that there is a prohibition of the means to *shirk* such as *tajsees* of graves (plastering them in order to make them into permanent structures),[1] building on top of them,[2] writing on them,[3] placing lights on them,[4] taking them as

---

[1] Based upon what is verified by Muslim and others that *"The Messenger of Allah ﷺ forbade that the graves should be plastered (made into permanent structures), used as sitting places (for the people) or building over them."* To know more about the position of Imām ash-Shāfi'ī and of many of his followers with regards to this issue refer to: *al-Muhadhdab*, vol.1, p.456; *Rawdat ut-Tālibeen*, vol.1, p.652; *al-Majmū'*, vol.5, p.266; *as-Sirāj ul-Wahhāj*, vol.1, p.114; *Sharh Muslim li'n-Nawawī*, vol.7, p.37-8 and *al-'Iqd uth-Thameen*, p.186.

[2] To know more about the position of Imām ash-Shāfi'ī and of many of his followers with regards to this issue refer to: *al-Muhadhdhab*, vol.1, p.456; *Rawdat ut-Tālibeen*, vol.1, p.652; *al-Majmoo'* vol.5, p.266; *as-Sirāj ul-Wahhāj*, vol.1, p.114 and *Sharh ul-Muslim li'n-Nawawī*, vol.7, p.307.

[3] Based on what was reported by Abū Dāwūd, at-Tirmidhī and others from the *hadeeth* of Jābir ؓ that the Messenger of Allāh ﷺ *"forbade that the graves should be plastered (made into permanent structures) and that they be written on."* To know more about the position of Imām Shāfi' ī and of many of his followers in regards to this issue refer to: *al-Umm*, vol.1, p.278; *Rawdat ut-Tālibeen*, vol.1, p.652; *al-Muhadhdhab*, vol.1, p.451; *al-Majmoo'*, vol.5, p.266; *as-Sirāj ul-Wahhāj*, vol.1, p.114 and *al-'Iqd uth-Thameen*, p.186.

[4] Based on the saying of the Prophet ﷺ *"Allāh has cursed women who visit graves, those who build masājid on them and those who erect lamps (over them)."* in order to know the position

masājid,[1] praying to them,[2] facing them in *duā',*[3] making *tawāf* around them,[4] sitting on them,[5] kissing them, touching them,[6] placing sun-shades

---

of the Shāfi'ī scholars on this issue refer to *az-Zawājir*, vol.1, p.194 and *Fath ul-Majeed*, p.186

[1] The Prophet ﷺ said: *"Allāh cursed the Yāhūd and the Nasārā because they took the graves of their prophets as Masājid."* The *hadeeth* is agreed upon. He ﷺ also said *"Those before you used to take the graves of their Prophets as Masājid, do not take graves as Masājid! I forbid you from doing that!"* Reported by Muslim and others. In order to know more about the position of the Shāfi'ī scholars in this regard refer to: *al-Umm*, vol.1, p.278; *Sharh Muslim li'n-Nawawī*, vol.5, pp.11-14 and *az-Zawājir*, vol.1, p.194

[2] Based on what is reported by Muslim and others that the Prophet ﷺ said, *"Do not sit on graves and to not pray on them."* In order to know more about the position of Imām Shāfi'ī and his followers in this regard refer to: *al-Umm*, vol.1, p.46; *Sharh Muslim li'n-Nawawī*, vol.7, p.38 and *az-Zawājir*, vol.1, p.194.

[3] Refer to the footnote above, to know more about the position of the Shāfi'ī scholars in this regard refer to *al-Mawdū'*, vol.8, p.257.

[4] Allāh says, **"...and perform tawāf around the ancient House."** {*al-Hajj (22): 29*} The one who makes *tawāf* around a grave in reality compares it to the House of Allāh the Haram which the Muslims make *tawāf* around. For more on the position of the Shāfi'ī scholars on this issue refer to *al-Majmū'*, vol.8, p.257; *az-Zawājir*, vol.1, p.194 and *Tatheer ul-Janān*, p.37.

[5] Based upon what is verified by Muslim and others that *"The Messenger of Allah ﷺ forbade that the graves should be plastered (made into permanent structures), used as sitting places (for the people) or that a construction be built on them."* In order to know more about the position of the Shāfi'ī scholars in this regard refer to Nawawī, *Sharh Muslim*, vol.7, p.37.

[6] It is well known that Allāh did not legislate for us to kiss any place specifically except for the *Black Stone* and He did not legislate for us to touch anything except for the *Black Stone* and the *Yemeni Corner*. As for what those people do at graves then such practices are extreme which lead to falling into *shirk* and innovation as it equalises between

over them,[1] to say *"by Allāh and by your beloved"*[2] or to say *"whatever Allāh and you will"*[3].

Imām ash-Shāfiʿī ﷺ said:

It is disliked to plaster graves and to write on them the name of the person within the grave and the likes. It is also disliked to build on them.[4]

The Imām also said:

I have seen from the leaders those of them who destroy whatever has been built on graves and the *Fuqahā* did not see any problem in what the leaders did.[5]

He also said:

---

sanctified symbols in Islām and graves. These are nothing but practices of those who are misguided yet think that they are actually guided. To know more about the position of the Shāfiʿī scholars in this regard refer to *al-Majmūʿ*, vol.8, p.257.

[1] The evidences against this have been mentioned in the previous footnotes, to know more about the position of the Shāfiʿī scholars in this regard refer to *al-Majmūʿ* vol.5, p.266.

[2] Based on the saying of the Prophet ﷺ: *"Whoever swears by other than Allāh has committed shirk."* See *Tafseer Ibn Katheer*, vol.1, p.101.

[3] Based on the saying of the Prophet *(sallAllāhu ʿalayhi wassallam)* *"You have made me a partner with Allāh"* which he said in reply to the person who said to him *"whatever Allāh and you want."* See *Tafseer Ibn Katheer*, vol.1, p.101.

[4] *Al-Majmūʿ*, vol.5, p.266

[5] *Al-Muhadhdhab*, vol.1, p.456

It is disliked to glorify the creation so that its grave becomes a *masjid*, this is out of the fear that it would be a *fitnah* for the person and for those people after him.[1]

Imām Nawawī said:

It is disliked to plaster graves and to build and write on them even if the grave is found within a cemetery it should be destroyed.[2]

Ibn Hajar al-Makkī al-Haytamī said:

The third, fourth, fifth, sixth, seventh, eighth and ninetieth major sin is to take graves as *masājid*, to place seats on them, to take them as idols, to make *tawāf* around them and to pray to them.

He also said:

All of these six from the major sins are found within the statements of some Shāfi'ī scholars and it is as if these (major sins) are taken from the ahādeeth, for the issue of taking a grave as a *masjid* for example is clear because he, meaning the Prophet ﷺ cursed whoever does that and he viewed the one who does that at graves to be of the worst of creation with Allāh on the day of Judgement. Within this therefore, is a warning for us as is found in the narration "*be warned of what they used to do*" meaning: he warned his Ummah, by his

---

[1] *As-Sirāj ul-Wahhāj*, vol.1, p.114

[2] *As-Sirāj ul-Wahhāj*, vol.1, p.114

words to them, to not do what those people before did and be cursed as they were cursed. Taking a grave as a *masjid* means to pray to on it or to it...and these graves are turned to if there is a Prophet or pious person within it as the narration indicates *"...if there was a pious man among them..."*

From here then our companions (from the Shāfiʿī madhhab) say: it is *harām* to pray to the graves of the Prophets and *Awliyā*, such as praying on them, *tabarruk* (seeking blessings) and glorifying them. The status of this action is that it is a manifest major sin as is evident from the aforementioned *ahādeeth*. It is as if all type of glorification of graves were intended: such as placing seats on graves out of glorification, seeking blessings *(tabarruk)* from them and likewise making *tawāf* around graves.

It was clearly mentioned in the aforementioned hadeeth that whoever places lamps over graves is cursed and as for the one who takes a grave as an idol then the forbiddance of that is found within his saying 🌸, *"Do not take my grave after me as an idol that is worshipped."* Meaning: do not praise it like other than you praised their idols by prostrating to them or the likes - up to where he said-: the worst of the prohibited actions and the means to *shirk* is to pray by it (i.e. the grave), take the grave as a *masjid* or build over it. The *'Ulama* do not permit this and it has been reported abundantly from the Prophet 🌸 that there is a curse for whoever does these actions.

141

These graves have to be destroyed along with the domes built over the graves as they are more harmful than *Masjid ad-Dirār* as they were built upon disobedience to the Messenger ﷺ because the Messenger forbade such things and instructed to destroy such graves and all candles or lights have to be removed from these graves and it is not correct to stand by them or make vows at them.[1]

An-Nawawī said:

It is not permissible to make *tawāf* around his (the Prophet's ﷺ) grave and it is disliked to stick ones front and back to the walls of the grave as has been stated by Abū 'Ubaydullāh al-Haleemī and others. They said: it is disliked to touch the grave and kiss it, rather it is from manners to be distant from it just as the people were distant from him when he was alive. This is what is right as the 'Ulama have emphasised and applied without being deceived by the contradictory practise of the common people and their actions. This is because guidance and action can only be via the authentic *ahādeeth* and the statements of the 'Ulama without turning to the newly invented novelties of the common people and others and their ignorant practices. From the danger of the one like this is that he touches the grave with his hand and the likes in order to attain *barakah* (blessings) yet this only shows the person's ignorance and

---

[1] *Az-Zawājir 'an Iqtirāf al-Kabā'ir*, vol.1, p.195

heedlessness as *Barakah* is only within that which agrees with the *Shar'*, so how can one seek virtue by that which opposes what is correct?[1]

Al-Baghawī said:

It is disliked to place a sun-shade over a grave because 'Umar ﷺ saw a sun-shade on a grave and instructed that it be removed.[2]

It is mentioned in Ibn Hajar's explanation of *al-Minhāj* and what has been abridged from it:

It is disliked to plaster graves, build over them and write on them due to the three authentic prohibitions against doing this. This is whether the name of the deceased or of someone else is written on it…

Al-Badāwī said, as is found within the notes of as-Suyūtī to *Sunan an-Nasā'ī*:

When the *Yāhūd* and *Nasārā* began to prostrate to the graves of their Prophets and turn to them in order to glorifying their status, make them a *Qiblah* to pray towards in *Salah*, make *du'ā* to them and take them as idols – Allāh cursed them and prevented the Muslims from

---

[1] *Al-Majmū'*, vol.8, pp.257-58
[2] *Al-Majmū'*, vol.5, pp.266

the likes of that. The origin of *shirk* is that it began from the glorification of graves and being turned towards (to worship).[1]

As-Suwaydī ash-Shāfi'ī said:

So you see them praise graves above all heights and write verses of the Qur'ān on them, make coffins out of sandalwood and ivory, place silk with pure gold and silver over these coffins. This was not enough to please them until they circulated these graves with windows made from silver and the likes. They then place golden candles around these graves and build golden or inscribed glass domes over them and they adorned doors (to these graves) with gold and then made silver locks for these doors out of fear of thieves. All of this opposed the *Deen* of the Messengers and is the source of enmity against Allāh and His Messenger. So if these people are really followers (of the *Deen*) they would look at what he (the Prophet ﷺ) did and what he used to do with his companions who were the most virtuous of followers. They would also look at his noble grave and what the Sahābah did in regards to it.[2]

An-Nawawī said:

The Prophet ﷺ only forbade that his grave, and the graves of others, be taken as *masājid* out of fear of exaggeration in glorifying him and

---

[1] *Hāshiyat Sunan an-Nasā'ī*, vol.2, p.42

[2] *Al-'Iqd uth-Thameen*, p.185

causing *fitnah* to the people, it is possible that this will lead to *kufr* as happened with many of the past nations. So when the Sahābah 📿 wanted to increase the size of the *masjid* of the Prophet 📿 due to the increase in the number of Muslims, the *masjid* was increased to include the houses of the mothers of the believers including the room of Ā'ishah 📿. If the Messenger of Allāh 📿 and his two companions, Abū Bakr and 'Umar 📿, were buried and a grave with encompassing raised walls was constructed over that and was manifest in the *masjid* that would have led to prohibited actions. They built two walls at the corners of the grave and diverted them in order to form a triangular angle to the north so that it was not possible for anyone to face the grave.[1]

It is mentioned in *al-Bā'ith fī Inkār al-Bida' wa'l-Hawādith* (p.103):

So look, may Allāh have mercy on you, and wherever you find a lote-tree or another tree that the people praise and glorify them, seeking intercession through them then that is a *Dhāt-Anwāt* so chop it down![2]

---

[1] *Sharh Saheeh Muslim*, vol.5, p.13-14

[2] [TN]: *al-Bā'ith fī Inkār al-Bida' wa'l-Hawādith* [An Inciter to Rejecting Innovation and Newly-Invented Matters] is authored by Abū Shāmah (d. 665 AH/1267 CE), a copy that it well known was printed in Cairo in 1955 CE, I am unaware of any other prints. It is also worth highlighting the role of Imām Abū Shāmah *(rahimahullāh)*:

Abū Shāmah was a Damascene Shāfi'ī scholar who was one of the Mujtahid scholars (according to his biographers) who emphasized returning to the Qur'ān and Sunnah; opposing bida' and assertin ijtihād for those qualified scholars. All of this was before Shaykh ul-Islām Taymiyyah who is erroneously held to be the "founder" of this Salafī trend after the epoch of the Salaf. Abū Shāmah's famous works include *Kitāb ur-Rawdatayn fī Akhbār id-Dawlatayn, Mukhtasar al-Mu'ammal fi'r-Radd ilā'l-Amr il-Awwal, al-Muhaqqaq min'Ilm il-Usūl fīmā yata'allaq bi Af'āl ir-Rasūl, al-Murshid al-Wajeez ilā 'Ulūm tata'allaqu bi'l-Kitāb il'Azeez.*

In *al-Mu'ammal* Abū Shāmah had a chapter entitled 'Section on the Obligation of Referring Back to the Qur'ān and Sunnah' wherein he highlighted that the Revelatory Texts have to take precedence in solving disputes in the religion. He also made reference to the statements of the earlier Imāms in regards to uncritical following of juristic views. Abū Shāmah also criticized his contemporaries for reliance on the later writings of Abū Ishāq ash-Shīrāzī (d. 1083 AH) and al-Ghazālī (d. 1111 AH), hence Abū Shāmah's emphasis on 'the first affair' as opposed to the developments that transpired within later generations. Konrad Hirschler states in his paper on Abū Shāmah:

> Abū Shāma's position was certainly a minority one in his time, as for him the process of ijtihād could never come to an end since no scholar could claim an authoritative status compared to the Quran and sunna. His position shows, contrary to the middle position discussed above, that ijtihād in its classical sense had not entirely come to an end in later centuries. Abū Shāma understood the term ijtihād as a direct return to the revealed sources. Although he certainly advanced no claims to founding a new madhhab, he refused to accept that the later authorities, such as the founders of the madhhabs, had an all-embracing hegemonic position.

Hirschler also states:

> Abū Shāma, for example, delivered a sharp criticism of his period around what he perceived to be the mujtahid/muqallid dichotomy.

See Konrad Hirschler, *Pre-Eighteenth Century Traditions of Revivalism: Damascus in the Thirteenth Century* (Bulletin of SOAS, vol.68, no.2, 2005), pp.202, 203.

ᴇᴈ Answering a Doubt ᴇᴈ

The grave-worshippers try to use the story of the Companions of the Cave whose people took their locations of death as a *masjid* as a proof for the permissibility of building *masājid* on graves. Al-Hāfidh Ibn Katheer answered this doubt in two ways:

1. This was an action of a idol-worshipping and disbelieving people so this in itself is not a proof.

2. Even if this was an action of Muslims, then they were not praised for doing this.[1]

---

[1] See *Tafseer Ibn Katheer*, vol.3, p.78. [TN] Look at the grave of Abu'l-Hasan ash-Shādhilī,which can be seen Online, as an example of a gross disregard of the consensus of Shāfi'ī scholars regarding graves.

⌐ Samples of Shirk Which the Shāfi'ī Scholars Have Cautioned Against ⌐

It has been transmitted from Imām ash-Shāfi'ī 🙏 and some of his companions that there is a prohibition of the types of major and minor *shirk*, such as: *duā'* and *istighātha* (seeking relief and help) from other than Allāh,[1]

---

[1] Based on Allāh's saying, **[Remember] when you asked help of your Lord, and He answered you, "Indeed, I will reinforce you with a thousand from the angels, following one another."** *{al-Anfāl (8): 9}* And Allāh saying, **"And your Lord says, "Call upon Me; I will respond to you." Indeed, those who disdain My worship will enter Hell [rendered] contemptible."** *{Ghāfir (40): 60}* And Allāh's saying, **"And who is more astray than he who invokes besides Allāh those who will not respond to him until the Day of Resurrection? And they, of their invocation, are unaware."** *{al-Ahqāf (46): 5}* And the Prophet 🙏 said: *"Verily du'ā is worship."* To know more about the statements of the Shāfi'ī scholars in regards to this issue refer to: Ibn Hajar al-Makkī, *al-I'lām bi-Qawāti' al-Islām*, p.95, 71; *al-'Iqd uth-Thameen* and *Tatheer ul-Janān*, p.38.

As for what some of them have narrated from ash-Shāfi'ī that he allegedly said *"If any severity befalls me I go to the grave of Abū Hanīfah and he answers."* Al-Alūsī al-Hanafi said:This is a lie and it is obvious that it is a lie to anyone who has any knowledge of transmission, because when ash-Shāfi'ī came to Baghdād there was no grave present in Baghdād at that time that was turned to for dua'a whatsoever. Rather, Abū Hanīfah was not that well known during his time and ash-Shāfi'ī had visited Hijāz, Yemen, Shām, al-'Irāq, Egypt which were all places wherein the graves of the Prophets, the Sahābah and the Tābi'īn were to be found and all of these were better than Abū Hanīfah and other scholars on his level. So why would *du'ā* only be made to Abū Hanīfah? Furthermore, the companions of Abū Hanīfah who met him such as Abū Yūsuf, Muhammad, Zafar, al-Hasan bin Ziyād and their likes were all not known to go to the grave of Abū Hanīfah and make *du'ā* there. Ash-Shāfi'ī made expressly clear in some of his books that it is disliked to exalt and glorify graves out of fear of the *fitna* that it would lead to. The ones who popularised the likes of these stories are those who have scant knowledge and *Deen* and these stories are only transmitted from those who are unknown *(majhūl)*. See *Fath ul-Mannān*, pp.372-73.

[TN]: The report is found in *Tārīkh Baghdād* by al-Khateeb al-Baghdādī and is from Qādī al-Husayn ibn 'Alī al-Saymarī who narrated to them, that the trustworthy *(thiqa)* Imam 'Umar ibn Ibraheem [ibn Ahmad] al-Muqrī told him, that the trustworthy Shaykh Makram ibn Ahmad told them, that 'Umar ibn Ishaq ibn Ibrahim told them, that the trustworthy Shaykh 'Ali ibn Maymūn told them: "*I heard al-Shāfi'ī say: 'I swear I seek the blessing of Abu Hanifa (inni la'atabarraku bi-Abi Hanifa) and come to his grave every day'* - meaning as a visitor – '*Whenever I have a certain need I pray two rak'ās then I come to his grave and ask Allah Most High for my need at his grave, and little time passes until it is fulfilled.*'" Narrated by al-Khateeb in *Tāreekh Baghdad* (vol.1, p.123) cf. al-Kawthari in his *Maqalat* (p. 453) and by Ibn Abi'l-Wafa' in *Tabaqāt al-Hanafiyyah* (p. 519) through al-Ghaznawi. Imām al-Haytamī cites it in the thirty-fifth chapter of his book on Imam Abu Hanifa entitled *al-Khayrat al- Hisan*. However, Imām al-Albānī highlighted that one of the persons in the chain, namely Umar bin Ishāq ibn Ibrāheem is *majhūl* thus rendering the report to be weak.

Imām al-Albānī said in his book *Silsilah al- Ahādeeth ad Da'eefah* (vol.1, p.31): '*This narration is weak, rather it is false. For verily Umar Ibn Ishāq Ibn Ibrāheem is unknown, and he is not mentioned in any of the books of Rijāl...*

Imām as-Suyūtī said in his book Tadreeb ur-Rāwī (p. 172): '*The majority of scholars do not accept the one who is unknown in terms of his 'Adalah whether open or secret.... and as for the one who is not known at all some who accept the narration of one who is unknown in terms of 'Adalah do not accept this type of narration (the one who is not known at all).*'

prostration to other than Allāh,[1] bowing to other than Allāh,[2] making vows to other than Allāh,[3] slaughtering to other than Allāh,[4] believing that

---

Ibn Katheer (Shaykh Ahmad Muhammad Shākir, ed.) said in his book Ikhtisār Ulūm ul-Hadeeth (p. 90): *'And as for the unknown person who is unnamed, or the one who is named and remains unknown, then he is from those that no one is known to accept narrations from.'*
Ibn Taymiyyah in Iqtidā Sirāt ul-Mustaqeem (p.165) also noted that this story is weak.

[1] Based on Allāh's saying, **"O Mary, be devoutly obedient to your Lord and prostrate and bow with those who bow [in prayer]."** *{Āli 'Imrān (3): 43}* In order to know more about the position of the Shāfi'ī scholars on this issue see: *Rawdat ut-Tālibeen*, vol.7, p.283-84; *al-Jamal 'alā Sharh il-Minhāj*, vol.5, p.124; *al-Mughnee ul-Muhtāj*, vol.4, p.136; *al-I'lām bi-Qawāti' il-Islām*, pp.19-21, 63, 93, 95, 98; *Tatheer ul-Janān*, p.37.

[2] Based on Allāh's saying, **"O Mary, be devoutly obedient to your Lord and prostrate and bow with those who bow [in prayer]."** *{Āli 'Imrān (3): 43}* In order to know more about the position of the Shāfi'ī scholars on this issue see: *Rawdat ut-Tālibeen*, vol.7, p.283-84; *al-Jamal 'alā Sharh il-Minhāj*, vol.5, p.124.

[3] Based on Allāh saying, **"Then let them end their untidiness and fulfil their vows and perform tawāf around the ancient House."** *{al-Hajj (22): 29}* Vows are worship which have to be for Allāh, for more on the views of the Shāfi'ī scholars in regards to this issue see: *al-Majmū'*, vol.8, p.435; *Mughnī ul-Muhtāj*, vol.4, p.371; *Tatheer ul-Janān*, pp.31, 37; *al-'Iqd uth-Thameen*, p.219; *Fath ul-Majeed*, p.213 and *Qurrat ul-'Uyyūn il-MuwahhiDeen*, pp.96, 86.

[4] Based on Allāh's saying, **"So pray to your Lord and sacrifice [to Him alone]."** *{al-Kawthar (108): 2}* And Allāh's saying, Say, **"Indeed, my prayer, my rites of sacrifice, my living and my dying are for Allāh, Lord of the worlds."** *{al-An'ām (6): 162}* Slaughtering is an act of worship which has to be only for Allāh, in the name of Allāh, it is not permissible to eat that which has been slaughtered without the name of Allāh being mentioned on it. For more on the views of the Shāfi'ī scholars in regards to this issue see: *Rawdat ut-Tālibeen*, vol.7, p.284; *az-Zawājir*, vol.1, p.168; *al-'Iqd uth-Thameen*, p.222 and *Tatheer ul-Janān*, p.37.

someone else other than Allāh knows the unseen,[1] swearing oaths to other
than Allāh,[2] saying *"whatever Allāh and you want"*[3] and believing that a
magician has an influence based on his own accord.[4]

Ash-Shāfi'ī said:

Whoever swears on oath by other than Allāh is like a man saying: *"By
the Ka'bah, by my father and by such and such a place"*. There is no
kaffārah for this and all oaths sworn to other than Allāh are disliked

---

[1] Based on Allāh saying, **"[He is] Knower of the unseen, and He does not disclose His
[knowledge of the] unseen to anyone…"** *{Jinn (72): 26}* Allāh also says, **"Say: 'None in
the heavens and earth knows the unseen except Allāh'…** *"{an-Naml (27): 65}* For more
on the views of the Shāfi'ī scholars in regard to this issue see: *al-I'lām bi-Qawāti' il-Islām*,
pp.69, 71; *al-'Iqd uth-Thameen* and al-Baghawī, vol.4, pp.405-406.

[2] Based on what the Prophet 鏺 said: *"Whoever swears by other than Allāh has committed
shirk."* And in another wording *"…has committed kufr."* To know the view of the Shāfi'ī
scholars in this regard see: *al-Umm*, vol.7, p.61; *al-Majmū*, p.19, 227-28; *Sharh us-
Sunnah*, vol.10, p.9; Ibn Daqeeq al-'Eid, *Ihkām ul-Ahkām*, vol.4, p.144; *Hilyat ul-'Ulama*,
vol.7, p.246; *Mughnī u-Muhtāj*, vol.4, p.324; *al-Jamal 'alā Sharh il-Minhaj*, vol.5, p.288;
Fath ul-Bārī, vol.11, p.530-31.

[3] Based on what the Prophet 鏺 *"Do you make me a partner will Allāh? Say: whatever Allāh
alone wills."* Which he said to the one who said to him: "whatever Allāh and you want."
To know the view of the Shāfi'ī scholars on this issue see: *Sharh us-Sunnah*, vol.12,
pp.360-61.

[4] Based on Allāh's saying, **"He said, "Throw," and when they threw, they bewitched the
eyes of the people and struck terror into them, and they presented a great [feat of]
magic."** *{al-A'rāf (7): 116}* And Allāh saying, **"What they have crafted is but the trick of a
magician, and the magician will not succeed wherever he is."** *{Tā Hā (20): 69}* For the
position of the Shāfi'ī scholars refer to *al-I'lām bi-Qawāti' il-Islām*, p.98

and prohibited based on the saying of the Messenger of Allāh ﷺ *"Allāh has forbidden you from swearing by your fathers, so whoever swears an oath then let him do it by Allāh or keep silent."*[1] Ibn 'Uyaynah informed us saying: az-Zuhrī narrated to us saying: Sālim narrated to us from his father saying: the Prophet ﷺ 'Umar swear by his father saying: *"Indeed, Allāh has forbidden you from swearing oaths by your fathers."* 'Umar ﷺ said: *"By Allāh I did not swear by that after that."*[2] All who swear by other than Allāh fall into that which is disliked and it is feared that his oath is one of disobedience.[3]

Ibn Hajar al-Haytamī al-Makkī said:

The 197th major sin: slaughtering in the name of other than Allāh.

Ar-Rifā'ī stated in *Sharh ul-Minhāj*:

As for making vows at the mausoleums of a *Walī*, Shaykh or to the name of the *Awliyā*, then if the one making the vow (as happens in

---

[1] Verified by al-Bukhārī, vol.11, p.530, *hadeeth* no.6646 in *Kitāb ul-Īmān wa'n-Nadhr, Bāb la Tahlafū bi-Ābāikum*; Muslim in *Kitāb ul-Īmān*, vol.3, p.1266, *hadeeth* no.1646 *Bāb an-Nahy 'an al-Halaf bi Ghayrillāh*; an-Nasā'ī, vol.7, p.4 in *Kitāb ul-Īmān, Bāb al-Halaf bi'l-Ābā*; Abū Dāwūd, vol.3, p.569, *hadeeth* no.3249 in *Kitāb ul-Īmān, Bāb fī Karāhoyat il-Halaf*.

[2] Verified by Abū Dāwūd, vol.3, p.570, *hadeeth* no.3250 in the book of *Īmān* chapter: *Karāhiyat ul-Halaf bi'l-Ābā*; an-Nasā'ī, *Kitāb ul-Īmān, Bāb ul-Halaf bi'l-Ābā*, vol.7, p.4, *hadeeth* no.2766; Ibn Mājah in *Kaffārāt*, vol.1, p.667, *hadeeth* no.2094 – from the narration of Sālim from his father from 'Umar ﷺ.

[3] *Kitāb ul-Īmān*, vol.7, p.61

most cases or generally) intends glorification of places, mausoleums or *zawiyas*;[1] or glorification of the one buried within the grave or is alleged to have been buried in the grave– then such a vow is void and is not conclusive. For their belief is that these places have a special status and that they prevent calamities, bring about blessings and intercede via vows made to them. To the extent that one makes vows to stones which were have been ascribed to a righteous worshipper, they also make vows to take saddles and oil to some graves and the people who do such things say: *"the grave of such and such to the place of such-and-such accepts vows that are made to it"* and they mean by this that such graves and places can give people the things that people hope for such as curing the sick, making the absent appear, obtaining wealth or anything of the likes of such types of vows. A vow like this is *bāṭil* (null and void) without doubt; rather making vows with oil and candles to graves is absolutely invalid.

Including in this is to make vows of abundant candles and the like to the grave of al-Khaleel Ibrāheem ﷺ and to the graves of other Prophets and *Awliyā*. For the one who makes vows at the graves of these does not do so except out of seeking blessings and glorification thinking that this is nearness to Allāh. There is no doubt that this is

---

[1] A Zāwiyah (pl. zawāyah) literally means "a corner" and is the term that is applied to a Sūfī hospice, a small mosque, a *musallah* or is mostly applied to a building which includes the tomb of a Sūfī. [TN]

falsehood and the lighting of candles at graves is *harām* whether one benefits from it or not.[1]

An-Nawawī says:

If one vows to go to a *masjid* other than the three *masājid* which are: *al-Masjid al-Haram*, Madeenah and *al-Aqsā*, then his vow is neither obligatory nor to be convened.[2]

Ibn Hajar al-Makkī said in *Sharh ul-Minhāj*:

"In the name of Allāh and Muhammad" is not to be said, this is prohibited due to associating partners as it is the right of Allāh only that slaughter is to be done in His Name. If one wants to slaughter in the Name of Allāh and seek blessings *(tabarruk)* in the name of Muhammad then this is just disliked.[3]

Ahmad bin Hajar al-Būtāmī ash-Shāfi'ī said in *Tatheer ul-Janān* (pp.31-32):

Meaning: they are not to make vows to other than Allāh, neither to the righteous nor *tawāf* around anything other than the Ancient House. It is not permissible to make vows to *Awliyā* or the righteous or to make *tawāf* around graves, as the ignoramuses do around the graves of al-Jīlānī, Husayn, al-Badawī, ad-Dusūqī and others - so all of this is *shirk* and there is no dispute about this. Many of the

---

[1] *Fath ul-Majeed*, p.213

[2] *Al-Majmū'*, vol.8, p.471

[3] Ibid.

ignorant innovators makes vows to the righteous and some of them send money (as vows) to the custodian (of the graves) or to reconstruct domes as many of the Indians and Pakistanis do when they make vows of money to Abdul-Qādir al-Jīlānī and for his tomb, this is from one who claims to be from Ahl us-Sunnah.

As for the Indian, Pakistani and Iranian *Shī'a*, then they make vows of wealth to the graves of Ahl ul-Bayt in Najaf, Karbalā', Khurasān and Qum and make arduous journeys to them from different parts of the world in order to make *tawāf* of those graves, seek relief from those who are within these graves and ask for the things that they want and (to) avert calamities – all of which only the Creator of the Heavens and the Earth is Able to grant. Likewise, it is not permissible to make a vow to a grave of a pious person and the graves of the righteous. So whoever makes a vow to other than Allāh does not have to fulfil it rather the person making the vow has to seek Allāh's forgiveness, repent to Him and say the Two Testimonies of faith again because the person was a *Murtad* if he knew that making a vow to other than Allāh is *shirk*.

As for what some of them say that *"the vow is for Allāh and the reward is for the Walī,"* then this is *bātil* and clear misguidance. If the person intended to give *sadaqah* then he should rather give *sadaqah* to the poor.

Also it is not known if the person in the grave was indeed a righteous person, and matters are judged by the end results so a person may have been truthful on the outside yet inside was a *zindīq*. Their lies are further manifest when they take sheep to these graves and slaughter them there and when they are criticised for these action they say *"the slaughter is for Allāh and the reward is for the Walī"*. The intent of this is nothing but chicanery and overturning the realities as they do not intend anything except the *Walī* as the *'Ulama* are frank in that no slaughtering should be made to Allāh in a place wherein slaughter to other than Allāh is made based on the hadeeth from Thābit bin ad-Dahhāk who said: A man made a vow to sacrifice a camel at a place called Buwanah, so he asked the Prophet (ﷺ) about it. He (ﷺ) said, "Did the place have any idol which is worshipped of the idols of Jahiliyah?" they answered "No." The Prophet ﷺ asked again *"Did the disbelievers hold any of their recurring festivities there?"* They answered "No." Allāh's Messenger ﷺ then said *"Fulfill your vow. Verily, there is neither fulfilment of a vow that is made in disobedience to Allāh nor one that is beyond a person's capacity."*[1]

---

[1] Hadeeth is verified in Abū Dāwūd, *Kitāb ul-īmān, Bāb mā yuʿam bihi min al-Wafāʾ bin-Nadhr*, vol.3, p.607, *hadeeth* no. 3313; al-Bayhaqī in his *Sunan*, vol.10, p.83; at-Tabarānī in *al-Kubrā* (*hadeeth* no. 1341) from the *hadeeth* Thābit bin ad-Dahhāk and authenticated by al-Hāfidh Ibn Hajar in *Talkhees ul-Khabeer*, vol.4, p.180.

Ahmad bin Hajar Āl Būtāmī ash-Shāfi'ī said in response to the doubts of the grave-worshippers:

Firstly: some of the ignorant say: those - meaning the grave-worshippers - believe in the Creator and in the Divine Legislation of Islam and the Day of Reward. Their main aim they say is to make *tawassul* by these dead righteous and they are not pleased with the title of shirk to be applied to them and rather they flee from this term, so how can it be said that they are *Mushrikūn*? Secondly, the (first) *Mushrikūn* committed *kufr* due to their rejection of *Rubūbiyyah* not due to their performing acts of worship to other than Allāh. They use as evidence for this the saying of Allāh,

$$﴿قَالُوا وَمَا الرَّحْمَنُ﴾$$

"...they say, And what is the Most Merciful?"

{al-Furqān (25): 60}

$$﴿وَهُمْ يَكْفُرُونَ بِالرَّحْمَــنِ﴾$$

"...while they disbelieve in the Most Merciful."

{ar-Ra'd (13): 30}

Al-Būtāmī answered with the following:

The answer to them being named as *Mushrikūn* is that *kufr* and *shirk* both has branches and types just as how *īmān* has branches. So if one comes with much from the branches of *īmān* and has alongside it some aspects from the branches of *shirk*, then it will be said that the person is a *Mushrik*. For example, even if he prays, fasts, believes in the Message and the Last Day and is known for *zuhd* and good manners, yet believes that the planets have an influence or that they have the ability to benefit or harm, or he believes in regards to an angel or a Messenger that which is not permissible to believe about them except in regards to Allāh and as a result we call such a person a *Mushrik* even if the person does some righteous actions.

These are the meanings mentioned in the issue of apostasy, so the ruling on a person with *kufr* or *shirk* is not necessitated except if the person falls into all of their aspects and types. Making *tawassul* by the righteous is due to their belief that they were sinful and as the dead pious people were closer to Allāh and can go between them and Allāh, this is precisely the *shirk* of the original Arabs. As for their utterance of the Two Testimonies (*Shahādatayn*) then this is negated by their actions which nullify them, just as how relieving oneself nullifies *wudū*. So their affirmation of the Creator does not benefit them at all because the *Mushrikūn* used to affirm *Rubūbiyyah* and this was not enough for to enter them into Islām. As for the saying of the one who says that: the *Mushrikūn* of the Arabs of old used to reject Resurrection, then the answer to this is: this belief is from that which is *kufr* and the Messenger of Allāh ﷺ judged them to have *kufr* and permitted their blood due to many matters, the most important of these matters is their worship of idols and their denial of the Resurrection. It is not acceptable for a person to believe in some parts and disbelieve in some parts rather it is obligatory to have belief in all that is found in the Qur'ān and what was brought and done by the Messenger of Allāh ﷺ. So whoever believes in some and does not believe in some parts is a disbeliever as Allāh has said about them,

﴿وَيَقُولُونَ نُؤْمِنُ بِبَعْضٍ وَنَكْفُرُ بِبَعْضٍ وَيُرِيدُونَ أَن يَتَّخِذُواْ بَيْنَ ذَلِكَ سَبِيلاً﴾

"...and say, "We believe in some and disbelieve in others," and wish to adopt a way in between." *{an-Nisā (4): 150}*

The mere utterance of the *kalima* of the *Shahādah* does not benefit them until they free themselves from all that which is worshipped other than Allāh and perform all acts of worship, whatever they maybe, to only Allāh.

However, can a specific person, or a specific group, be made *takfeer* of for their nullifiers of *tawheed* and *kufr* even though they believe in Allāh and the Messenger and perform all of the Divine Legislation?

The answer: it can be said that such actions are those of *shirk* and *kufr* such as: *sujood* to a *Walī*, *tawāf* around a grave, making a vow to a grave, however, as for a specific person or group then we do not immediately make *takfeer* of them rather we have to inform them of the verses of the Qur'ān and the *ahādeeth* of the Messenger of Allāh ﷺ which clarify *shirk* and warn from it. We also have to clarify that the person who commits such *shirk* will have no portion of Paradise whatsoever and that these actions are *shirk*. So if a specific person or group continues in this way (of falling into *shirk*) and is stubborn and does not accept, then at this point it is permitted to apply *shirk* to them. If a specific person differentiates between major and minor *shirk*, such as *riyā'* then this is minor *shirk*, while *sujūd* to other than Allāh is major *shirk*. So if one was to say *"your words necessitate making takfeer of most of the Ummah of Muhammad because they do that which you call shirk such as making vows to Awliyā and the likes"* then the answer to this is:

a.	General statements are different from specific statements.

b.	Ignorance is rife and knowledge of *tawheed* and the purified Sunnah is scant. As is understanding of *shirk*, its categories and its means within many places and countries.

These prevent *shirk* from being applied to a specific individual, except for the one to whom the texts have reached and upon whom the proofs have been established and still persists on *shirk* out of stubbornness – such an individual is judged to have *shirk*.[1]

The answer to the second doubt:

The first Āyah

﴿قَالُوا وَمَا الرَّحْمَنُ﴾

---

[1] *Al-'Aqā'id as-Salafiyyah bi-Adilatiha an-Naqliyyah wa'l-'Aqliyyah*, pp.37-40.

161

"…they say, And what is the Most Merciful?"

{al-Furqān (25): 60}

…is a question from The Most-Merciful and asking about something is not rejection of it…

As for the second Āyah,

$$﴿وَهُمْ يَكْفُرُونَ بِالرَّحْمَـٰنِ﴾$$

"…while they disbelieve in the Most Merciful."

{ar-Ra'd (13): 30}

…then this refers to *kufr* in ar-Rahmān and disbelief in something is not rejecting it, so for example you say about someone who does an action of *kufr* "*so-and-so has disbelieved*" and this indicates that he has rejected the Lord.

From here it is clear to us that the Shāfi'ī scholars warn from *shirk* and its harmful consequences in this life and the next, *Allāh is the One we ask for help and upon Him we rely.*

⊰ Conclusion ⊱

All praise is due to Allāh who has helped us to finish this and this is all due to Allāh's Blessing and Virtue and all praise is due to Him and from the most important results from this work have been the following:

1. The speech of Imām Shāfi'ī and his early companions were scarce in regards to the innovation of the grave-worshippers due to the fact that grave-worship had not become widespread during their time. Whereas the later followers of Imām Shāfi'ī had much speech in regards to condemning grave-worship.

2. Many of the Shāfi'ī *'Ulama* had admirable efforts in preventing the means to *shirk* and safeguarding *tawheed*.

3. The innovations related to graves lead to many people falling into major *shirk*.

4. The range of precautions within the Divine Legislation which preserve *tawheed* and prohibit all means which lead to *shirk* such as those actions that are connected to glorifying graves.

5. The range of individual humiliations connected to *shirk* due to worshipping other than Allāh and due to *shirk* corrupting the individual's mind by believing in legends and superstitions.

This is a small effort, which I ask Allāh to accept as something sincerely for His Noble Countenance. Apologies to the readers due to any shortcomings, and weakness is a feature of the son of Adam.

Shirk According To Scholars From

The Hanbalī Madhhab

⊰ Introduction ⊱

This is the fourth book from the series *An Explanation of Shirk and the Means to it*. The first in the series looked at the explanations given by the Hanafī scholars, while the second was according to the Mālikī scholars and the third was according to the Shāfi'ī scholars. This, the fourth in the series, is related to the explanation of shirk and the means to it according to the Hanbalī scholars.

I have maintained that I shall not quote anything from Shaykh ul-Islām Ibn Taymiyyah, his student *al-'Allāmah* Ibn ul-Qayyim or from Imām Muhammad ibn 'AbdulWahhāb I and his offspring. This is because I desired to show the concern of this serious issue with the Hanbalī scholars and to avoid it seeming as if those scholars mentioned have a monopoly on the subject and went into the issue the most, to the extent that some of the ignoramuses attach issues related to 'aqeedah to 'Wahhābism' and the likes.

From what has been clearly proven is that many people have been deceived by what has said about the Imāms of *da'wah* throughout the ages and what has been ascribed to them.

Muhammad Rasheed Ridā ﷺ[1] said:

When we were young we used to hear stories about the 'Wahhābīs' based on the articles of Dahlān and other similar tracts. We used to believe them as we followed our Shaykhs and fathers and we believed that the Ottoman state was the maintainer of the *Deen* and this was the reason for why they fought against them (so-called 'Wahhābīs') and kept them in check. Yet I did not know the reality of this group (i.e. the so-called 'Wahhābīs') except after my *hijrah* to Egypt when I came across the History of al-Jabartī[2] and the *Kitāb ul-Istiqsā fī Akhbār il-Maghrib il-Aqsā.*[3] After which I came to realise from these books that they (the so-called 'Wahhābīs') were upon the correct Islamic guidance as opposed to those who they were fighting against...[4]

---

[1] He is Muhammad Rasheed bin 'Ali Ridā bin Muhammad ShamsuDeen al-Qalamūnī al-Baghdādī, originally "al-Hasanī". He was the editor of *al-Manār* magazine and was one of the men of the Islamic revival. He was born and educated in Tarāblus (in Shām) and died in Cairo in the year 1354 AH, see *al-A'lām*, vol.6, p.126 and *Mu'jam ul-Mu'aliffeen*, vol.9, p.310.

[2] He is 'AbdurRahmān bin Hasan al-Jabartī, the *Muftī* of the Hanafis during the time of Muhammad 'Ali Khadīwī. He died in 1237 AH, refer to *al-A'lām*, vol.3, p.304 and *Mu'jam ul-Mu'alliffeen*, vol.5, p.133.

[3] *Kitāb ul-Istiqsā'* is the work by Ahmad bin Khālid an-Nāsirī ad-Dar'ī as-Salāwī, a historian and researcher. He died in the year 1315 AH, refer to *al-A'lām*, vol.1, p.120 and *Mu'jam ul-Mu'alliffeen*, vol.1, p.214.

[4] *Muqaddimah Kitāb Siyānat il-Insān*, p.8

The Hanābilah: are those who are ascribed to the *madhhab* of respected Imam, Ahmad bin Muhammad bin Hanbal ﷺ in the subsidiary branches of *fiqh*. He is one of the four Imams that are followed and he was the core of the *Deen* and distanced himself from the leaders and the rulers, he came out defending the truth and for the sake of Allāh did not fear the blame of the blamers. He died ﷺ in 241 AH after being tested with the inquisition which he was patient with and Allāh raised him in rank due to that tribulation. He was also made an Imām and leader of the *'Ulama*.

◄ Definition of Shirk According to Some Hanbali Scholars ►

Before we commence in explaining *shirk* and its definition according to the Hanbalī *'Ulama*, we will explain the meaning of *shirk* within the Arabic language.

Sha-ri-ka: meaning to become a partner who has a share in something. The verbal nouns (*masdar*): *shirk*, *sharikah* and *mishrikah*. "*Ashrakahu fee amrihi*" ("he shared with him in the matter"): means he joined in it with him. "*shārakahu*" ("he joined him"): meaning he was his partner. Sharraka baynahum ("he joined them together"): means he made them partners. As for the definition according to the *Hanābilah* then they have differed in their terms of expression in defining *shirk* even though its main meaning is one.

Ibn Rajab said:

> To make the creation assume the same level as the Creator to be worshipped, it is therefore to put something not in its proper place. Most of what is mentioned in the Qur'ān threatening the transgressors is referring to the *Mushrikūn* as Allāh ﷻ said,

$$﴿وَالْكَافِرُونَ هُمُ الظَّالِمُونَ﴾$$

171

"The disbelievers are transgressors" *{al-Baqarah (2): 254}*[1]

Ibn Rajab said in defining minor *shirk* as being *riyā'* (showing off):

> The people who have *riyā'* have a greater punishment over other
> sinners because *riyā'* is minor shirk and sins that are connected to
> *shirk* are worse than other sins.[2]

He indicated what the intent of hidden *shirk* was when he said:

> All blessing are from Allāh and His Virtue, so whoever ascribes any
> of these blessings to other than Allāh with the belief that it is not
> from Allāh is a real *Mushrik,* and whoever ascribes these blessings to
> other than Allāh with the belief that they are from Allāh has
> committed hidden *shirk.*[3]

The Muftī of the Hanbalīs in Makkah of his time, Shaykh Abū Bakr bin
Muhammad 'Ārif Khuqayr[4] stated:

> *Shirk* is to compare the creation with the Creator in regards to
> Divine Characteristics that are unique to Allāh. In other words: it is
> to believe that other than Allāh has an influence over what Allāh has

---

[1] *Jāmi' ul-'Ulūm wa'l-Hikam,* vol.2, p.181

[2] *At-Takhweef min an-Nār,* p.223

[3] *Latā'if ul-Ma'ārif,* p.70

[4] He is Abū Bakr bin Muhammad 'Ārif bin 'AbdulQādir bin Muhammad bin 'Ali
Khuqayr al-Makkī, a Hanbalī *faqeeh* who was born in Makkah in the year 1282 AH, he
died in the year 1349 AH. Refer to his biography in *al-A'lām,* vol.2, p.70 and *Mu'jam ul-
Mu'alliffeᵢn,* vol.3, p.73.

given it, and that something has authority which is outside the ability of the creation.[1]

He also said:

Shirk is to make other than Allāh have the same control, *Rubūbiyyah* is from Him to His servants and worship from His servants is for Him.

Abū Bakr bin Muhammad bin al-Hanbalī said:

Shirk is the worse disease to afflict a person, it is when a person is set up as a partner with Allāh and this is contrary to *tawheed*. For that reason, I advise myself and every Muslim male and female to know *shirk* in order to stay away from it, in this way our Lord says,

﴿إِنَّ اللَّهَ لاَ يَغْفِرُ أَن يُشْرَكَ بِهِ وَيَغْفِرُ مَا دُونَ ذَلِكَ لِمَن يَشَاء وَمَن يُشْرِكْ بِاللّهِ فَقَدِ افْتَرَى إِثْمًا عَظِيمًا﴾

"Indeed, Allāh does not forgive association with Him, but He forgives what is less than that for whom He wills. And he who associates others with Allāh has certainly fabricated a tremendous sin." *{an-Nisā (4): 48}*

And He also says,

﴿إِنَّهُ مَن يُشْرِكْ بِاللّهِ فَقَدْ حَرَّمَ اللّهُ عَلَيهِ الْجَنَّةَ وَمَأْوَاهُ النَّارُ﴾

---

[1] *Kitāb mā lā buda minhu*, p.30

"Indeed, he who associates others with Allāh – Allāh has forbidden him Paradise, and his refuge is the Fire. And there are not for the wrongdoers any helpers." *{al-Mā'idah (5): 72}*[1]

---

[1] *Al-'Aqeedah fī Safahāt*, p.39

⊰ The Categories of Shirk According to the Hanbalī Scholars ⊱

Shirk opposes *tawheed* and it is obligatory for a Muslim to know the major and minor categories of *shirk* along with its apparent and hidden types in order to stay away from them and keep his *deen* safe. Yet this is not done except with understanding of these different categories and the means to them and the ways to prevent them. As was clear from the explanation of Ibn Rajab mentioned prior about *shirk* it is clear that there are three categories of *shirk*: major, minor and hidden. Abū Bakr bin Muhammad bin al-Hanbalī said:

Firstly: major *shirk* is the category which necessitates being placed into Hellfire for eternity and expulsion from the religion of Islām. It has six types under it which will be listed below by the will of Allāh:

1 – *Shirk* of *du'ā*: to make *du'ā* to other than Allāh whether it be to Prophets and Awliyā asking them for provision, cures or anything else, this is based on what Allāh says

﴿ وَلاَ تَدْعُ مِن دُونِ اللَّهِ مَا لاَ يَنفَعُكَ وَلاَ يَضُرُّكَ فَإِن فَعَلْتَ فَإِنَّكَ إِذًا مِّنَ الظَّــلِمِينَ ﴾

"And do not invoke besides Allāh that which neither benefits you nor harms you, for if you did, then indeed you would be of the wrongdoers." *{Yūnus (10): 106}*

2 – *Shirk* of intention, want and intention: this is doing righteous actions for a worldly aim alone, Allāh says about this,

﴿ إِنِّي تَوَكَّلْتُ عَلَى اللَّهِ رَبِّي وَرَبِّكُمْ ۚ مَّا مِن دَابَّةٍ إِلَّا هُوَ ءَاخِذُۢ بِنَاصِيَتِهَا ۚ إِنَّ رَبِّي عَلَىٰ صِرَٰطٍ مُّسْتَقِيمٍ ﴾

"Whoever desires the life of this world and its adornments – We fully repay them for their deeds therein, and they therein will not be deprived. Those are the ones for whom there is not in the Hereafter but the Fire. And lost is what they did therein, and worthless is what they used to do." *{Hūd (11): 15-16}*

3 – *Shirk* of love (*mahabbah*): to love one of the *Awliyā* as one should love Allāh,[1] this is based on what Allāh says,

﴿ وَمِنَ ٱلنَّاسِ مَن يَتَّخِذُ مِن دُونِ ٱللَّهِ أَندَادًا يُحِبُّونَهُمْ كَحُبِّ ٱللَّهِ ۖ وَٱلَّذِينَ ءَامَنُوٓاْ أَشَدُّ حُبًّا لِّلَّهِ ﴾

---

[1] This speech is not that detailed and it would have been better for him to have said "Loving other than Allāh as one should love Allāh" based on the general meaning of the ayah in this issue.

"And [yet], among the people are those who take other than Allāh as equals [to Him]. They love them as they [should] love Allāh. But those who believe are stronger in love for Allāh." {al-Baqarah (2): 165}

4- *Shirk* of obedience *(ta'a)*: to obey the *'Ulama* and Shaykhs in sin when they make *istihlāl*, based on when Allāh says,

﴿اتَّخَذُوا أَحْبَارَهُمْ وَرُهْبَانَهُمْ أَرْبَاباً مِّن دُونِ اللَّهِ وَالْمَسِيحَ ابْنَ مَرْيَمَ﴾

"They have taken their scholars and monks as lords besides Allāh, and [also] the Messiah, the son of Mary."
{at-Tawbah (9): 31}

5 –*Shirk* of incarnation *(hulool)*: this is the belief that Allāh is incarnate within His creation, like the belief of Ibn 'Arabī as-Sūfī who is buried in Damascus, and of others.

6 – *Shirk* of control: it is the belief that some of the *Awliyā* have an influence in the universe and can control affairs, such as the beliefs about the *Aqtāb* and *Abdāl*.[1] This is even though Allāh asked the *Mushrikūn* of the past,

---

[1] [TN] these are terms used within Sufism which are applied to individuals who are given qualities which are only within the domain of Allāh.

﴿قُلْ مَن يَرْزُقُكُم مِّنَ السَّمَاءِ وَالْأَرْضِ أَمَّن يَمْلِكُ السَّمْعَ وَالْأَبْصَـــرَ وَمَن يُخْرِجُ الْحَيَّ مِنَ الْمَيِّتِ وَيُخْرِجُ الْمَيِّتَ مِنَ الْحَيِّ وَمَن يُدَبِّرُ الْأَمْرَ فَسَيَقُولُونَ اللَّهُ﴾

"Say, 'Who provides for you from the heaven and the earth? Or who controls hearing and sight and who brings the living out of the dead and brings the dead out of the living and who arranges [every] matter?' They will say, 'Allāh,'..." *{Yūnus (10): 31}*[1]

Before we go to the statements regarding types of major *shirk* it is worth us taking a look at how to avoid falling into this dangerous matter. One way is to avoid saying *"we have received rainfall due to the such-and-such a planet"* wherein one says this believing that a planet has an influence in bringing rain – this is *kufr* because it is *shirk* in *Rubūbiyyah*. If one says this, but without believing in it, the person has committed minor *shirk* as he has ascribed the blessing of rain to other than Allāh.

Minor *shirk* does not expel the one who commits it from the *deen*, Abū Hurayrah ﷺ narrated: I heard the Messenger of Allāh ﷺ say, *"The first person to be decreed upon on the Day of Judgment will be a martyr. When he will be brought, Allāh will recount his blessings, which he will acknowledge. Allāh will ask him, "So how did you react to them?" He will say, "I fought for You until I was martyred." Allāh will say, "You*

---

[1] *Al-'Aqeedah fee Safahāt*, p.40-41

have lied. You fought so that you would be called a brave man, which you were called." Then he will be ordered to be dragged away on his face into the fire. The second will be a person who studied and taught knowledge and the Qur'ān. When he will be brought, Allāh will recount his blessings, which he will acknowledge. Allāh will ask him, "So how did you react to them?" He will say, "I studied and taught the knowledge and read the Qur'ān for Your sake." Allāh will say, "You have lied. You studied knowledge so that you would be known as a scholar and you recited the Qur'ān so that you would be known as reciter, which you were called." Then he will be ordered to be dragged away on his face into the fire. The third will be a person who Allāh had made rich and granted abundant wealth. When he will be brought, Allāh will recount his blessings, which he will acknowledge. Allāh will ask him, "So how did you react to them?" He will say, "I spent for Your sake for every cause for which You liked the money to be spent." Allāh will say, "You have lied. You did that so that you would be known as generous, which you were called." Then he will be ordered to be dragged away on his face into the fire."[1]

We will put forth some examples so as to explain some types of *Riyā'* in detail:

1 – Slight *Riyā'*:

---

[1] Reported by Muslim, vol.3, p.1514, *Kitāb ul–Imārah, hadeeth* no.1905

To act falsely for the sake of the creation, like a Muslim who acts for Allāh and prays to Allāh however perfects his prayer and actions so that the people praise him, Allāh says,

﴿فَمَن كَانَ يَرْجُو لِقَآءَ رَبِّهِ فَلْيَعْمَلْ عَمَلاً صَـــلِحاً وَلاَ يُشْرِكْ بِعِبَادَةِ رَبِّهِ أَحَدَا ﴾

"So whoever would hope for the meeting with his Lord – let him do righteous work and not associate in the worship of his Lord anyone..." *{al-Kahf (18): 110}*

The Prophet ﷺ said: *"What I fear for you the most is minor shirk, ar-riyā. Allāh will say on the Day of Judgement when He is rewarding the people for their actions: Go to those for whom you did riyā for in the dunya then see if you find the reward with them."*[1]

2 - Other types of *Riyā'* are:

A – *Riyā'* of the body: to manifest leanness and paleness to be seen as being from the servants (of Allāh) who exert themselves in worship and have fear of the Hereafter. Also included in this is to speak with a quiet voice, lower the gaze and manifest withered body to show that he is a person who fasts regularly.

B – *Riyā'* in one's clothing and appearance: such as to keep marks of prostration on the face and wearing specific forms of clothing which are associated with *'Ulama* so that it be said that he is a scholar.

---

[1] Reported by Ahmad in his *Musnad*, vol.5, pp.478-479 and others, al-Albānī authenticated it in *Saheeh ul-Jāmi'*, vol.1, p.323, hadeeth no.1555.

C – *Riyā'* in speech: this is the most common form of *Riyā'* among people associated with the *Deen* when they admonish, remind others, memorise narrations so as to manifest this in debates and show off knowledge, to move the lips as if in remembrance of Allāh, to manifest anger at evil actions committed by people, to lower the voice when reading the Qur'ān in order to show fear, grief and the like.

D – *Riyā'* of action: such as someone praying a lengthy prayer wanting to be seen, lengthening *rukoo', sujūd* and manifesting fear. It also includes wanting to be seen as a person who fasts, fights, makes Hajj, gives charity and the likes.

E – *Riyā'* in companionship and visitors: such as the one who safeguards visiting a scholar or a pious worshipper so that it be said "such-and-such has visited so-and-so". Or the one who calls the people to visit a certain scholar or worshipper so that it be said "the people of *deen* frequent him."

Therefore, *Riyā'* is included as being minor *shirk*, and for that reason swearing oaths to other than Allāh is included as being minor *shirk* for that reason the Prophet ﷺ said: *"Whoever swears an oath to other than Allāh has disbelieved or committed shirk."*[1]

---

[1] Related by Ahmad in *al-Musnad*, vol.2, p.69, 86; Abū Dāwūd, vol.3, p.569, *hadeeth* no.3251 in *Kitāb ul-Imān, Bāb fi Karāhiyat il-Halaf*; at-Tirmidhī, *Kitāb un-Nudhoor wa'l-Imān, Bāb Mā Jā fi Karāhiyyat il-Halaf bi Ghayrillāh*, vol.4, p.110, hadeeth no.1535; al-Bayhaqī in *as-Sunan*, vol.10, p.29; al-Hākim, *al-Mustadrak*, vol.1, p.18. All of these

3 - Hidden Shirk:

Ibn 'Abbās ⬥ explained this as being when a man says to his friend *"whatever Allāh and you will"* and *"if not for Allāh and such and such"* when rather it is correct for him to say *"if not for Allāh and then such-and-such"* and *"Whatever Allāh wills and then what you will."* Also to say *"I seek refuge in Allāh and you"* and *"I trust in Allāh and you."* Rather it should be said *"I seek refuge in Allāh and then you"* and *"I trust in Allāh and then you"* and so on. From Abū Sa'eed in a *marfū'* form who said: the Messenger of Allāh ⬥ said, *"Shall I not inform you of what I fear for you more than the maseeh ud-dajjāl? It is hidden shirk. It is when a man stands up for prayer, then beautifies his prayer for another to look at."*[1] The expiation for minor and hidden *shirk* is for a man to say: *"O Allāh I seek refuge in You from me associating anything*

---

reports are via Sa'd bin 'Ubaydah from Ibn 'Umar and the wording with at-Tirmdhī and al-Bayhaqī is: *"Whoever swears by other than Allāh has disbelieved or committed shirk."* The wording in al-Hākim is *"Whoever swears by other than Allāh has disbelieved."* At-Tirmidhī stated: "This hadeeth is hasan", al-Hākim said "this hadeeth based on the conditions of Shaykhayn is credible with such an isnād" and adh-Dhahabī agreed with this in *at-Talkhees*.

[1] Ibn Mājah, vol.2, p.1406, 4204 in *Kitāb uz-Zuhd, Bābur-Riyā' wa's-Sum'ah*, from the hadeeth of 'AbdurRahmān bin Abī Sa'eed al-Khudrī from his father in *marfū'* form. Al-Albānī deemed the hadeeth to be *hasan* in *Saheeh ul-Jāmi'*, vol.1, p.509, hadeeth no.2607.

in worship with You while we know, and we ask for Your forgiveness of what we do not know."[1]

I say: pay attention to his categorisation of *shirk* as it includes Riyā' as being minor *shirk* just as Ibn Rajab did. From the people of knowledge are those who include swearing oaths to other than Allāh as being minor *shirk* along with saying "*If Allāh and you wills*" and the likes. Hidden *shirk* is *Riyā'* and there is no problem with this as all views have their respective evidence. Also pay attention that he was heedless of other types of *shirk* such as *shirk* of fear, hope, trust and other types. It would have been better for him to have included them and to have said *shirk* in *Uboodiyyah* and to explain all of the types of worship which are *ishrāk* with Allāh.

Al-'Allāmah Abū Bakr Muhammad bin 'Ārif Khuqayr, the Muftī of the Hanābilah in Makkah, divided *shirk* into six categories:

1 – Shirk in Independence (Istiqlāl):[2] affirming two independent gods like the *shirk* of the Magians

2 – Shirk in Division (Tab'īdh): which is extracting a god from another god, like the *shirk* of the Christians

---

[1] *Al-'Aqeedah fī Safahāt*, pp.39, 43, 45.

[2] This does not exist, refer to *Sharh ut-Tahawiyyah* by Ibn Abi'l-'Izz, p.19, for the Magians do not associate partners in worship in *shirk* in independence and there is none in the world who commits this type of *shirk*, so this is a mistake that has to be highlighted.

3 – Shirk in Nearness (Taqreeb): worshipping other than Allāh in order to gain nearness to Him.

4 - Shirk of *Taqleed*:[1] like the *shirk* of the later people of the times of *Jāhiliyyah*

5 - Shirk in Causes (Asbāb): to ascribe causes to other than the Power of Allāh as the philosophers and atheists do when they say "it rained due to the planet tempest"

6 - Shirk in Needs (Aghrādh): doing actions for other than Allāh and this is judged as being sinful as some of the scholars have mentioned.[2]

I say: it is apparent from this categorisation that the author did not extract the categories of *shirk* that arrived in the *Shari'* texts, rather he focused on *shirk* in *Rubūbiyyah* and *Ulūhiyyah* and did not highlight *shirk* in the Attributes. We can sometimes find *'Ulama* who focus on a specific aspect due to widespread errors and misconceptions in regards to it and some focus on other aspects.

---

[1] In his explanation of this it would have been better to say "*shirk* in *taqleed* by following the *'Ulama* and rulers in a matter that opposes the Divine Legislation."

[2] *Kitāb Mā Lā Budda Minhu*, p.31

⫷ Means to Shirk Which the Hanbalī Scholars Have Cautioned Against ⫸

Imām Ahmad bin Hanbal ﷻ attached the utmost importance to the issue of preventing the means (*dharā'i*). This is confirmed from him as al-Qurtubī said:

Holding firm to preventing the means and safeguarding this is the *madhhab* of Imām Mālik and his companions and Ahmad bin Hanbal.[1]

It has arrived from Imām Ahmad ﷻ and some of his followers that they forbade the means that lead to *shirk* such as plastering over graves (in order to make them permanent structures),[2] building over them,[3] writing on

---

[1] *Tafseer ul-Qurtubī*, vol.2, pp.57-58

[2] It is reported in Muslim from Jābir said: *"The Messenger of Allah ﷺ forbade that the graves should be plastered (made into permanent structures), used as sitting places (for the people) or built over."* Ibn Qudāmah said: *'Because that is from the adornment of the dunya and the dead have no need for that whatsoever.'* To know more about the position of the Hanbalī scholars on this matter refer to: *Kashāf ul-Qinā'*, vol.2, p.139; *al-Kāfī*, vol.1, p.270; *al-Mubdi'*, vol.2, p.273; *al-Muqni'*, vol.1, p.285; *al-Mu'tamid*, vol.1, p.249 and *al-Mughnī*, vol.3, pp.439-440.

[3] The evidence for the prohibition of this is the previous hadeeth and also the hadeeth that Abu'l-Hayāj al-Asadī said: 'Ali ibn Abi Tālib ﷺ said to me: *"Shall I not send you with*

them,[1] taking them as *masājid*,[2] facing them when making *du'ā*,[3] prostrating to them, praying by them,[4] kissing them,[1] using *bukhūr* by them,[2] placing

---

the same instructions as the Messenger of Allāh 鑿 *sent me? 'Do not leave any image without defacing it or any built-up grave without levelling it.'"* To know more about the position of the Hanābilah on this matter refer to *Kashāf ul-Qinā'*, vol.2, p.138; *al-Mubdi'*, vol.2, p.272; *al-Mu'tamid*, vol.1, p.249; *al-Mughnī*, vol.3, p.435. Ibn Qudāmah said about the word *'mushrifa' (tomb): mushrifa is a type of grave that has been raised to a high level and the evidence for this is the statement of Ibn ul-Qāsim and his companions in describing the grave of the Prophet* 鑿: *it was not a mushrifa.*

[1] Based on what was reported by Abū Dāwūd, at-Tirmidhī and others from the *hadeeth* of Jābir 鑿 that the Messenger of Allāh 鑿 *'forbade that the graves should be plastered (made into permanent structures) and that they be written on.'* To know more on the position of the Hanbalī scholars on this issue refer to: *al-Muqni'*, vol.1, p.285; *al-Kāfi*, vol.1, p.270; *Kashāf ul-Qinā'*, vol.2, p.139; *al-Mubdi'*, vol.2, p.273; *al-Mu'tamid*, vol.1, p.249 and *al-Mughnī*, vol.3, pp.439-440.

[2] Based on the Prophet's 鑿 saying: *"Allāh cursed the yahood and the nasārā because they took the graves of their prophets as Masājid."* The *hadeeth* is agreed upon. He also said *(sallAllāhu 'alayhi wassallam): "Those before you used to take the graves of their Prophets as Masājid, do not take graves as Masājid! I forbid you from doing that!"* Reported by Muslim and others. Refer to: *al-Kāfi*, vol.1, p.267; *Kashāf ul-Qinā'*, vol.2, p.140; *al-Mu'tamid*, vol.1, p.250 and *al-Mughnī*, vol.2, p.475.

[3] Based on what was reported by Abū Ya'lā al-Mawsilī from 'Ali bin al-Husayn that he saw a man who used to go the grave of the Prophet 鑿 and made du'ā there so he forbade the man from doing it saying that the Prophet 鑿 said: *"Do not take my grave as a place of festivity"* and as-Sakhāwī deemed the hadeeth to be *hasan* in *al-Qawl ul-Badī'* (p.155). Refer to: *Kashāf ul-Qinā'*, vol.2, pp.150-151.

[4] Based on what has been reported by Muslim and others that the Prophet 鑿 said, *"Do not sit on graves and to not pray on them."* Refer to *Kashāf ul-Qinā'*, vol.2, pp.150-151; *al-Mubdi'*, vol.2, p.274 and *al-Mughnī*, vol.3, p.441. Ibn Qudāmah said: *'This is because*

lamps on them,[3] sitting on them,[4] placing pavilions and tents over them,[5] covering them,[6] making *tawāf* around them,[1] seeking cures for diseases at them,[2] touching them,[3] and travelling to them.[4]

---

specifying graves for prayer resembles veneration of idols by prostrating to them and gaining nearness to them. The worship of idols began by venerating the dead by taking their images and then touching them and praying to them.'

[1] See *Kashāf ul-Qinā'*, vol.2, p.140; *al-Mu'tamid*, vol.1, p.249 and *al-Mughnī*, vol.5, p.468.

[2] See *al-Mu'tamid*, vol.1, p.249

[3] Based on the saying of the Prophet ﷺ: *"Allāh has cursed women who visit graves, those who build masājid on them and those who erect lamps (over them)."* Reported by at-Tirmidhī, Ibn Mājah and others. Ibn Qudāmah said in *al-Mughnī: If it was allowed then the Prophet ﷺ would not curse those who do it, (and he cursed it) because it is a waste of money and is extremism in venerating graves which is similar to venerating idols.* In order to know about the position of the Hanbalī scholars refer to: *Kashāf ul-Qinā'*, vol.2, p.141; *al-Mubdi'*, vol.2, p.274; *al-Mu'tamid*, vol.1, p.250 and *al-Mughnī*, vol.3, p.440.

[4] Based on what has been reported by Muslim and others that the Prophet ﷺ said, *"Do not sit on graves and to not pray on them."* Refer to: *al-Kāfi*, vol.1, p.270; *al-Mubdi'*, vol.2, p.274; *Kashāf ul-Qinā'*, vol.2, p.139-140 and *al-Mughnī*, vol.3, p.440. It was mentioned to Imām Ahmad that Imām Mālik interpreted the hadeeth of the Prophet ﷺ to mean that he forbade using graves as places to relieve oneself, Imām Ahmad said *"this is nothing"* and was not pleased with this view of Mālik. Sitting on them is not actually a means to shirk but it is forbidden to sit on them so as not to disrespect cemeteries so it is better to say *"sitting by them"* such as resting on them or leaning up against the graces.

[5] See *al-Mubdi'*, vol.2, p.273; *Kashāf ul-Qinā'*, vol.2, p.139; *al-Mughnī*, vol.3, p.516.
Imām Ahmad disliked placing pavilions over graves and Abū Hurayrah on his death bed advised that a pavilion not be built over his grave.

[6] See *Kashāf ul-Qinā'*, vol.2, p.139

---

[1] Based on Allāh saying, "...**and perform tawāf around the ancient House.**" {*al-Hajj (22): 29*} Whoever makes *tawāf* around other than the House of Allāh, the *Harām*, resembled the place to the *Harām* and it is venerating what Allāh has not permitted by glorifying them. This is legislating in the *Deen* that which Allāh has not permitted and leads to *shirk* with Allāh and a person changing his *Deen*. To know more on the position of the Hanbalī scholars on this issue refer to: *Kashāf ul-Qinā'*, vol.2, p.140.

[2] The one who cures (ash-Shāfī) is Allāh and anyone seeking to be cured should ask Allāh along with taking the legislated means when seeking to be cured. The one who claims to cure people with the dust from graveyards is an innovator who has done what Allāh has not legislated and believes in cures and blessings from that which has no Divinely Legislated proof to cure. It is feared for such an individual that they have fallen into committing *shirk* with Allāh wherein he believes that the dust from the graveyards, and the graveyards themselves, can possible have an effect in benefitting or harming. This type of *shirk* is very dangerous and to know more on this refer to: *Kashāf ul-Qinā'*, vol.2, p.140.

[3] Because this compares graves to the Black Stone which Allāh Legislated to be touched, so seeking to touch it is legislating in the *Deen* other than what Allāh has allowed, to know more on the position of the Hanbalī scholars on this issue refer to: *Kashāf ul-Qinā'*, vol.2, p.150 and *al-Mughnī*, vol.5, p.467.

[4] Travelling to specifically visit places connected to the *deen* other than the three main *masājid* (Haram al-Makkī, Masjid an-Nabawī and Masjid ul-Aqsā) is *harām* based on what was said by the Prophet ﷺ: *"It is not befitting to travel (specifically) to any masjid except three: Masjid ul-Harām, my Masjid and Masjid ul-Aqsā."* Agreed upon. Refer to: *Sharh uz-Zarkashī* on the *Mukhtasar* of al-Kharqī, vol.7, p.211; *Kashāf ul-Qinā'*, vol.2, p.150 and *al-Mughnī*, vol.3, p.117.

⊰ Samples of Shirk That Have Been Mentioned and Cautioned Against by the Hanbalī Scholars ⊱

It has arrived from Imām Ahmad and some of his followers that there is a prohibition of various types of major and minor *shirk* such as: *du'ā* to other than Allāh,[1] *istighātha* (seeking help) from other than Allāh,[2] making vows to other than Allāh,[3] swearing oaths to other than Allāh,[4] having complete

---

[1] Allāh says, **"And your Lord says, "Call upon Me; I will respond to you." Indeed, those who disdain My worship will enter Hell [rendered] contemptible."** {Ghāfir (40): 60} And Allāh says, **"And do not invoke besides Allāh that which neither benefits you nor harms you, for if you did, then indeed you would be of the wrongdoers."** {Yūnus (10): 106} Refer to: *al-Furū'*, vol.6, p.165; *al-Muqni'*, vol.4, pp.152-153 and *Kashāf ul-Qinā'*, vol.6, p.168.

[2] Allāh says, **[Remember] when you asked help of your Lord, and He answered you...** {al-Anfāl (8): 9} To know more about the position of the *Hanābilah* on this issue refer to the previously mentioned references.

[3] As Allāh says, **"Then let them end their untidiness and fulfil their vows and perform tawāf around the ancient House."** {al-Hajj (22): 29} Making vows are acts of worship and worship is not befitting except unto Allāh, so making vows to other than Allāh is associating partners with Allāh. Refer to *Kashāf ul-Qinā'*, vol.2, p.151 and *al-Mu'tamid*, vol.2, pp.503-504.

[4] Based on the statement of the Prophet ﷺ: *"Whoever swears by other than Allāh has disbelieved or committed shirk."* Reported by Ahmad (vol.2, pp.67, 125) and others. Refer to: *Sharh uz-Zarkashī* on *Mukhtasar ul-Kharqī*, vol.7, pp.64 and 76; *al-Muqni'*, vol.4,

trust on other than Allāh,[1] prostrating to other than Allāh,[2] slaughtering to other than Allāh,[3] believing that someone other than Allāh knows the Unseen realm,[4] or believing that other than Allāh can control the universe,[5]

---

p.201; *al-Ifsāh*, vol.2, pp.320 and 323; *al-Kāfī*, vol.4, p.376; *al-Furū'*, vol.6, p.340 and *al-Mu'tamid*, vol.2, pp.483-484.

[1] Allāh says, **"And upon Allāh let the believers rely."** *{Ibrāheem (14): 11}* And Allāh says, **"...And upon Allāh rely, if you should be believers."** *{al-Mā'idah (5): 23}* Trusting other than Allāh is to avert worship to other than Allāh and this is *shirk*, for more on this topic according to the Hanābilah refer to: *al-Furū'*, vol.6, p.165; *al-Muqnī'*, vol.4, pp.152-153 and *Kashāf ul-Qinā'*, vol.6, p.168.

[2] Allāh says, **"O Mary, be devoutly obedient to your Lord and prostrate and bow with those who bow [in prayer]."** *{Āli 'Imrān (3): 43}* Prostrating to other than Allāh is associating partners in worship with Allāh and averting worship to other than Him, refer to: *al-Mubdi'*, vol.9, p.172; *al-Muqni'*, vol.4, pp.152-153; *al-Furū'*, vol.6, p.165 and *Kashāf ul-Qinā'*, vol.6, p.169.

[3] Allāh says, **"So pray to your Lord and sacrifice [to Him alone]."** *{al-Kawthar (108): 2}* Refer to: *al-Kāfī*, vol.1, pp.479-482; *al-Mughnī*, vol.8, p.568; *Sharh uz-Zarkashī* on *Mukhtasar ul-Kharqī*, vol.6, pp.667-670.

[4] Based on when Allāh says, **"[He is] Knower of the unseen, and He does not disclose His [knowledge of the] unseen to anyone..."** *{al-Jinn (72): 26}* For more from the *Hanābilah* on this issue refer to: *al-Muqni'*, vol.4, p.162; *Kashāf ul-Qinā'*, vol.6, p.69; *al-Mu'tamid*, vol.2, p.449 and *al-Mughnī*, vol.12, p.305.

[5] Allāh says, **"Say, [O Muhammad], "Invoke those you claim [as deities] besides Allāh." They do not possess an atom's weight [of ability] in the heavens or on the earth, and they do not have therein any partnership [with Him], nor is there for Him from among them any assistant. And intercession does not benefit with Him except for one whom He permits."** *{Saba (34): 22-23}* See: *al-Muqni'*, vol.4, p.195 and *al-Mughnī*, vol.12, p.301.

or believing that the planets (or the stars) have an effect in (determining the future).[1]

He (Ahmad) stated, as reported in *al-Iqnā'* and its *Sharh*:

Whoever puts between him and Allāh intermediaries and places complete trust on them and calls on them has disbelieved in the *ijmā'* because that is like the action of the idol-worshippers.[2]

Imām Abu'l-Wafā' 'Ali bin 'Aqeel al-Hanbalī[3] said:

Whoever venerates graves and calls upon the dead for his needs to be responded to by saying (for example) *"O my master 'AbdulQādir do this for me"* is a disbeliever in this case and whoever calls upon the dead and asks for their needs to be responded to is a disbeliever.[4]

---

[1] Based on what Allāh stated in the hadeeth *qudsī*: *"As for the one who says "we have been given rain on account of such and such a planet" then the person who says this is a disbeliever in Me and a believer in the planets."* Reported by al-Bukhārī and Muslim. Seeking nearness to the planets is seeking nearness to other than Allāh and believing that it can benefit, harm and have an influence and this is the most severest form of disbelief. Refer to: Ibn Hubayrah, *al-Ifsāh*, vol.2, p.226 and *al-Mughnī*, vol.12, p.301.

[2] Vol.6, p.168

[3] He is 'Ali bin 'Aqeel bin Muhammad bin 'Aqeel al-Baghdādī al-Hanbalī, his *kunyah* is Abu'l-Wafā', adh-Dhahabī said about him: *"Imām, al-'Allāmah, the ocean of knowledge, the Shaykh of the Hanābilah."* He died in the year 513 AH, refer to *Siyar A'lām un-Nubalā'*, vol.19, pp.443-451.

[4] *Hukmullāh al-Wāhid as-Samad*, p.44

Ibn 'Aqeel al-Hanbalī also said:

> When the responsibilities (of the *Shar'*) became difficult for the ignorant people they abandoned the constraints of the *Shar'* and gloried circumstances that they themselves had made up in order for it to be easy for them so that they would not fall under the order of anyone else besides themselves. I regard these people as *kuffār* for what they do in these circumstances such as venerating graves and speaking to the dead, asking for their needs to be answered by the dead and writing on pieces of paper "*O my master do such-and-such for me*" and piercing holes on trees following the way of the ones who worship al-Lāt and al-'Uzza.[1]

He also said in the book *al-Funūn*:

> Allāh has dignified the creatures, especially the son of Ādam in that He has allowed you to make *shirk* if compelled to do so and put the sanctity of you before the sanctity of Him to the extent that He has allowed you to mention Him with that which is not befitting to Him when you have to protect yourself. Allāh has dignified your honour by legislating the *hadd* punishment on the one who slanders you. Allāh has dignified what you own by legislating that the Muslim who steals from you should have his hand cut. Allāh has lessened the portion of prayer on you during travel; Allāh has established wiping

---

[1] *'Aqeedat ul-MuwahhidDeen*, p.64

of the socks to take the place of washing the feet as a concession to you in order to avoid the difficulty of removing your clothes; Allāh has allowed for you to eat the dead animals in order to keep your body well and to preserve your health; Allāh warns you from that which will harm you sooner and the threat that will come later; Allāh does what is beyond ordinary for your sake and Allāh revealed the Books unto you. So after this respect unto you, is it good for Him to see you going towards that which He has prohibited unto you? When He instructs you, you pay no attention and ignore it; when He warns you from something, you take no notice and commit it and you turn away when He calls you. It is not befitting for this noble, living and respected creation, over the rest of the creatures, to be seen as anything else than a worshipper of Allāh.[1]

Ibn Rajab[2] stated:

---

[1] *Kitāb ul-Funoon*, as mentioned in *'Aqeedat ul-MuwahhidDeen*, pp.64-65.

[2] He is ZaynudDeen 'AbdurRahmān bin Shaykh al-Imām al-Muqri' al-Muhaddith ShihābudDeen Ahmad bin Shaykh al-Imām al-Muhaddith Abī Ahmad Rajab 'AbdurRahmān al-Baghdādī and then ad-Dimishqī, well known as: Ibn Rajab al-Hanbalī. Ibn ul-'Imād said about him: *"The Imām, the 'Ālim (scholar), al-'Allāmah, az-Zāhid (ascetic), al-Qudwat ul-Barakah, al-Hāfidh (memoriser), al-'Umdah, ath-Thiqah (trustworthy), al-Hujjah (the proof), Hanbalī in madhhab."* He died in the year 795 AH. Refer to: *Shadharāt udh-Dhahab*, vol.6, pp.339-340 and Ibn Hajar, *ad-Durar al-Kāminah*, vol.2, pp.427-428.

The statement of the servant (of Allāh) "*la ilaha il Allāh*" indicates that he has no other god except Allāh, for a god is that which is obeyed and not disobeyed, and to whom glory, love, fear and hope is shown, and who is trusted, asked and supplicated to; and all of this is not correct except when given unto Allāh. So whoever associates the creation as having a share in these matters, which are specifically Divine Characteristics of Allāh has damaged his sincerity in saying "*la ilaha il-Allāh*" and has a deficiency in his *tawheed*. For this would be worship of the creation and that is a branch of *shirk* and for this reason the ascriptions of *kufr*[1] and *shirk* are applied to many acts of disobedience which are based on obeying other than Allāh or fearing,

---

[1] As is found in the hadeeth: "The contract between us and them is the prayer so whoever leaves the prayer has disbelieved." Reported by Ahmad in *al-Musand*, vol.5, p.346; Ibn Abī Shaybah in *al-Imān* (46); at-Tirmidhī; an-Nasā'ī; Ibn Hibbān; al-Hākim and others – from the hadeeth of Buraydah ﷺ in *marfū'* form and al-Albānī authenticated it in *Saheeh ul-Jāmi'*, vol.2, p.760, hadeeth no.4143. In the same way it is verified in another hadeeth: *"Abusing a Muslim is sin and fighting against him is kufr."* Reported by al-Bukhārī, vol.1, p.135, hadeeth no.48 in *Kitāb ul-Imān, 'Bāb Khawf ul-Mu'min min an yahbat 'Amalahu'* [Chapter: A Muslim's Fear of his Actions Being Rendered Worthless] – from the hadeeth of Abū Wā'il from Ibn Mas'ood in a *marfū'* form. It was reported by Muslim also and others. It is also verified in another hadeeth: *"Whoever swears on oath by other than Allāh has disbelieved or committed shirk."* Reported by Ahmad, vol.1, p.125; Abū Dāwūd, vol.3, p.570; at-Tirmidhī, vol.4, p.110 and al-Hākim, vol.1, p.52 who said that the hadeeth is saheeh according to the conditions of Shaykhayan. Adh-Dhahabī agreed with him and al-Albānī authenticated it in *Saheeh ul-Jāmi'*, vol.2, p.1067, hadeeth no.6204.

194

hoping and trusting in others and doing actions for other than Him.
So for example *shirk* has been applied to *Riyā'*,[1] to swearing oaths to
other than Allāh,[2] trusting other than Allāh, depending upon other
than Allāh. Believing Allāh to be the same with the creation is like
saying for example *"whatever Allāh and so-and-so wills"*.[3] Likewise
from the things which violate *tawheed* are: believing in omens,[4]
believing in disliked recitations for healing,[5] going to soothsayers and

---

[1] As is relayed in the hadeeth: *"Whoever prays to be seen has committed shirk and whoever gives charity to be seen has committed shirk and whoever fasts to be seen has committed shirk."* Reported by Ahmad in the *Musnad*, vol.4, p.126; at-Tabarānī in *al-Kabeer*, vol.7, p.337 and al-Hākim, vol.4, p.329, all of them authenticated the hadeeth from Shadād bin Aws.

[2] Refer to the hadeeth related to this which has been mentioned prior.

[3] As the Prophet ﷺ said to the one who said to him: "Whatever Allāh wills and you will!" The Prophet ﷺ said to him: *"Are you making me a partner with Allāh? Do not do that, rather say "whatever Allāh wills" alone."* Reported by Ahmad in the *Musnad*, vol.3, p.253. Ahmad Shākir said: "Its isnād is Saheeh". It was also reported by Ibn Mājah, vol.1, p.684 and at-Tabarānī in *al-Kabeer*, vol.12, p.244.

[4] As when the Prophet ﷺ said: *"Whoever lets tiyarah (superstitious beliefs in bird omens) stop him from doing something has committed shirk."* Reported by Ahmad, vol.2, p.220; at-Tabarānī and others, and it was authenticated by al-Albānī in *Saheeh ul-Jāmi'*, vol.2, p.1075, hadeeth no.6264 and it is from the hadeeth of 'Abdullāh bin 'Amru bin al-'Ās in *marfū'* form.

[5] As is found in the hadeeth: *"Indeed ruqā, tamā'im and tiwalah is shirk."* Reported by Ahmad in the *Musnad*, vol.1, p.381; Abū Dāwūd, vol.4, p.212; Ibn Mājah, vol.2, p.1167 and al-Hākim, vol.4, p.217 who authenticated it from the hadeeth of Ibn Mas'ūd ؓ in a *marfū'* form.

[TN] *Ruqā* is the practice of reciting incantations or charms. *Tamā'im* are amulets and talismans which are sometimes put around necks or hung around the home to ward off

believing in what they say,[1] following personal desires in what Allāh has prohibited – then all of this violates the completeness and perfection of *tawheed*.[2]

Then Ibn Rajab said:

So whoever loves something that Allāh hates, or hates something that Allāh loves, has not perfected his *tawheed* or his truthfulness in saying "*la ilaha il-Allāh*". Such a person has within him hidden shirk in accordance with what he hates of the things which Allāh loves and what he loves of the things which Allāh hates.[3] Allāh says,

---

evil. If these contain verses of the Qur'ān then some of the *Salaf* allowed this while others prohibited this such as Ibn Mas'ūd who disapproved of the practice. *Tiwalah* is witchcraft and bewitchment wherein people claim that they can prepare a potion or another strange occult practice in order to get a wife to increase loving her husband for example. This is very common in the Muslim world and some of those involved in this despicable trade will spend their time trying to gain customers than praying in the *masjid*.

[1] As is mentioned in the hadeeth: *"Whoever goes to a sorcerer or a diviner and believers in what he says, has disbelieved in what has been revealed unto Muhammad."* Ahmad, *Musnad*, vol.2, p.429 and al-Hākim from the hadeeth of Abū Hurayrah ﷺ in a *marfū'* form, al-Albānī authenticated it in *Saheeh ul-Jāmi'*, vol.2, p.1031, hadeeth no.5939.

[2] Allāh says, **"Have you seen he who has taken as his god his [own] desire, and Allāh has sent him astray due to knowledge and has set a seal upon his hearing and his heart and put over his vision a veil? So who will guide him after Allāh? Then will you not be reminded?"** *{al-Jāthiyah (45): 23}*

[3] In the hadeeth *"Whoever loves for Allāh, hates for Allāh, gives for Allāh and withholds for Allāh has perfected imān."* Reported by Abū Dāwūd, vol.5, p.60, hadeeth no.4681 in *Kitāb us-Sunnah*, '*Bāb ad-Daleel 'alā Ziyādat il-Imān wa Nuqsānuhu*' [Chapter: Evidence for the

﴿ ذَلِكَ بِأَنَّهُمُ اتَّبَعُواْ مَا أَسْخَطَ اللَّهَ وَكَرِهُواْ رِضْوَانَهُ فَأَحْبَطَ أَعْمَلَهُمْ ﴾

"That is because they followed what angered Allāh and disliked [what earns] His pleasure, so He rendered worthless their deeds." *{Muhammad (47): 28}*

Al-Layth said from Mujāhid in regards to the saying of Allāh,

﴿ يَعْبُدُونَنِي لَا يُشْرِكُونَ بِي شَيْئًا ﴾

"...[for] they worship Me, not associating anything with Me."
{an-Nūr (24): 55}

(That its interpretation is:) "That they do not love other than Me." In the *Saheeh* of al-Hākim[1] from 'Ā'ishah ؤ from the Prophet ﷺ that he said: *"Shirk in this Ummah is more hidden than a black ant crawling on a stone on a dark night."*[2] Like one loving something

---

Increases and Decrease of Imān] – from the hadeeth of Abū Umāmah in *marfū'* form. Al-Albānī authenticated it in *Saheeh ul-Jāmi'*, vol.2, p.1034, hadeeth no.5965.

[1] To ascribe this term *"Saheeh ul-Hākim"* is a greatly going beyond bounds as the book of al-Hākim contains that which is Saheeh and that which is not.

[2] Al-Hākim, vol.2, p.291 from the hadeeth of 'Urwah from 'Ā'ishah and al-Hākim said that the hadeeth has a *saheeh isnād*. Adh-Dhahabī said in his *Talkhees*: *'AbdulA'lā is in the chain of transmission and ad-Dāraqutnī said: he is not thiqah (trustworthy).* Al-Albānī authenticated the first part of the hadeeth in *Saheeh ul-Jāmi'*, vol.1, p.693, hadeeth no.3730.

which is unjust yet hating something which is just, and is the *Deen* anything but loving and hating? Allāh says,

﴿قُلْ إِن كُنتُمْ تُحِبُّونَ اللَّهَ فَاتَّبِعُونِى يُحْبِبْكُمُ اللَّهُ﴾

"Say, [O Muhammad], "If you should love Allāh, then follow me, [so] Allāh will love you..." *{Āli-'Imrān (3): 31}*

This indicates that love of what Allāh hates and hate of what He loves is following one's desires, and allegiance and enmity on that is hidden *shirk*.[1]

Al-'Allāmah Abū Bakr bin Muhammad Khuqayr mentioned in his book *Mā Lā Budda Minhu* some samples of *shirk* which the Prophet ﷺ cautioned against in order to safeguard *tawheed*, such as:

1. Using incantations for healing and amulets other than the Qur'ān[2]

2. Seeking blessings from trees, stones and the likes.[1]

---

[1] *Kalimat ul-Ikhlās* found within *Majmū' ur-Rasā'il al-Kamāliyyah*, vol.18, p.19 and vol.22, p.23.

[2] As is found in the hadeeth: *"Indeed ruqā (incantations), tamā'im (amulets and talismans) and tiwalah (bewitching and witchcraft) is shirk."* Its verification has been mentioned prior. Imām Ahmad ﷺ said: *"All of that it disliked and ruqā (incantations) which use verses of the Qur'ān are no problem."* Refer to *Masā'il ul-Kawsaj*, vol.2, p.169. Imām Ahmad also said about treating the one who is *majnoon* and has fits with *ruqā* and *azā'im*: *"It is more beloved to a person to do it, yet it is more beloved to me to leave it."* Refer to *al-Ahkām us-Sultāniyyah*, p.308.

3. Slaughtering to other than Allāh.[2]

4. Making vows to other than Allāh.[3]

---

[1] Seeking blessing from trees, stones and the likes are means to *shirk* and the Prophet ﷺ said when some of the Sahābah wanted to hang their swords on a tree for blessing as the Mushrikūn did: *"Allāh is Greater – and in another narration – Glory be to Allāh – Indeed it is a just a custom you said, I swear by the One Who has my soul in His hands, just as the people of Mūsā said to Mūsā, "...***Make for us a god just as they have gods...***""* {*Sūrah al-A'rāf (7): 138*} Reported by at-Tirmidhī, vol.4, p.475, hadeeth no.2180 in *Kitāb ul-Fitan, 'Bāb Mā Jā' li-Tarkabunna Sunan'* and at-Tirmidhī said: "the hadeeth is hasan saheeh"; Ibn Mājah in his *Saheeh*, vol.8, p.248, hadeeth no.6667; Abū Ya'lā, *Musnad*, vol.2, p.159; al-Humaydī, *Musnad*, vol.2, p.375, hadeeth no.848; Ibn Jareer, *Tafseer*, vol.9, p.45; at-Tayalisī (1346); Ibn Abī 'Āsim, *as-Sunan*, vol.1, p.37, hadeeth no.76; al-Lālikā'ī, *Usool ul-'Ttiqād*, vol.1, p.124, hadeeth no.204-205; at-Tabarānī, *al-Kabeer* – all from the hadeeth of Abū Wāqid al-Laythī in *marfū'* form and the hadeeth is Saheeh. Imām Ahmad rejected those who would touch his body with their hands in order to seek blessings from him, when this was done to Imām Ahmad he became angered and said *"Who did you get this from?"* He firmly and sternly rejected this practice, refer to *Tabaqāt ul-Hanābilah*, vol.1, p.228 and al-*Minhaj ul-Ahmad*, vol.1, p.428.

[2] The Prophet ﷺ said: *"Allāh cursed those who slaughter to other than Allāh..."* reported by Muslim, vol.3, p.1567, hadeeth no.1978 in *Kitāb ul-Adāhī* [Book of Slaughtering], *'Bāb Tahreem adh-Dhibh li-Ghayrillāh'* [Chapter: The Prohibition of Slaughtering to Other than Allāh] – from the hadeeth of Abu't-Tufayl from 'Ali and other also reported it. Imām Ahmad forbade eating meat which had been slaughtered to other than Allāh and was stern on this matter, refer to: *al-Masā'il wa'r-Rasāil al-Marwiyah'an il-Imām Ahmad bin Hanbal fi'l-'Aqeedah* [Issues and Transmitted Treatises from Imām Ahmad bin Hanbal Regarding 'Aqeedah], vol.129, p.131.

[3] It is well-known that making vows are acts of worship and it is not befitting that worship be directed to anyone except Allāh, Allāh says, **"They [are those who] fulfill**

5. Seeking refuge in other than Allāh.[1]

6. Seeking help from other than Allāh and making *du'ā* to other than Him.[2]

7. Seeking intercession via other than Allāh.[3]

8. Extremism in regards to the dead pious and over-praising them.[4]

[their] vows..." {al-Insān (76): 7} Allāh also says, **"Then let them end their untidiness and fulfil their vows and perform tawāf around the ancient House."** {al-Hajj (22): 29}

[1] Seeking refuge is turning to something and protection and it is not permissible to seek this from anyone except Allāh, Allāh says in His Book, **"So when you recite the Qur'ān, [first] seek refuge in Allāh from Satan, the expelled [from His mercy]."** {an-Nahl (16): 98} And Allāh also says, **"And if there comes to you from Satan an evil suggestion, then seek refuge in Allāh. Indeed, He is the Hearing, the Knowing."** {Fussilat (41): 36} Maryam ﷺ said, **"Indeed, I seek refuge in the Most Merciful from you, [so leave me], if you should be fearing of Allāh."** {Maryam (19): 18}

[2] It is not permissible to call on help and assistance from the creation in matters which only Allāh has ability over, Allāh says, **[Remember] when you asked help of your Lord, and He answered you...** {al-Anfāl (8): 9} And Allāh says, **"...while they call to Allāh for help..."** {al-Ahqāf (46): 17} So none but Allāh is called to (in *du'ā*) because *du'ā* is worship as is verified that Allāh says, **"And your Lord says, "Call upon Me; I will respond to you." Indeed, those who disdain My worship will enter Hell [rendered] contemptible."** {Ghāfir (40): 60}

[3] Allāh says, **"And intercession does not benefit with Him except for one whom He permits."** {Saba (34): 23} And Allāh also says, **"Say, "To Allāh belongs [the right to allow] intercession entirely."** {Zumar (39): 44}

[4] As the Prophet ﷺ prohibited that he be venerated: *"Do not venerate me as the Christians venerated Ibn Maryam, I'm only a servant (of Allāh) so say: Abdullāh wa Rasooluahu ('the servant of Allāh and His Messenger')."* reported by al-Bukhārī, vol.6, p.551, hadeeth no.3445 in the Ahādeeth of the Prophets, 'Chapter: the saying of Allāh "Mention in the

9. Worshipping at the graves of the dead pious.[1]

10. Magic and soothsaying/fortune-telling.[2]

11. Superstitious belief in omens.[3]

---

book Maryam"', from the hadeeth of Ibn' Abbās from 'Umar in *marfū'* form. So when the Prophet 🙵 prohibited that he be venerated it is also to be applied to others initially.

[1] Regarding this issue there are many *ahādeeth* forbidding taking graves as *masājid* and cursing those who do, also the forbiddance of taking the graves of the Prophets as *masājid* and these *ahādeeth* are verified in the Two Saheehs.

[2] Allāh says, **"It was not Solomon who disbelieved, but the devils disbelieved, teaching people magic..."** *{Baqarah (2): 102}* The *Kāhin* (soothsayer/fortune-teller) is the one who claims to have knowledge of the unseen realm of existence and is a disbeliever because he no one knows the unseen realm of existence except Allāh. Allāh says, **"Say, 'None in the heavens and earth knows the unseen except Allāh...'"** *{an-Naml (27): 65}* Imām Ahmad G was asked: *"Is the Kāhin (soothsayer/fortune-teller) more evil than the Sāhir (magician)?"* Imām Ahmad replied: *"All of them are evil!"* Relayed by Khallāl in *Ahkām Ahl il-Milal*, p.208. Imām Ahmad was also asked about the magician and said: *"If he is known for magic then I view that he should be executed."* Refer to *Masā'il 'Abdullāh bin Ahmad*, p.427. Imām Ahmad also said *"The Kāhin (soothsayer/fortune-teller) claims to know the unseen while the magician blows on knots."* Refer to *Ahkām Ahl il-Milal*, p.208.

[3] It is mentioned in a hadeeth: *"Whoever is turned away from what he needs to do because of an omen has committed shirk."* Its verification has been mentioned prior, *tatayyur* (believing in omens) is pessimism of a specific thing such as a specific day, a specific bird, a specific number or anything else.

[TN] Such as superstitious beliefs that are popular in the West about "Friday the 13th" (which in itself is nonsense for a Muslim to believe in as Friday, the day of Jumu'ah is a virtuous day!); superstitions regarding magpies and different amounts of them that are seen are supposed to bring good luck or bad luck (!); and superstitions about the numbers 7 and 13 – believing in these ridiculous superstitions which are based on the pagan idolatry of Europe is *shirk*.

12. Calling upon the planets for rain.[1]

13. Loving and fearing other than Allāh as one should love and fear Allāh.[2]

14. *Riyā'* and doing actions in order to gain what one wants in the dunya.[3]

---

[1] In the hadeeth: *"He who said we were rained upon by the mercy and generosity of Allāh is a believer, and he who said we were rained upon by the planets is a blasphemer of me and a believer in the planets."* Reported by al-Bukhārī, vol.2, p.388, hadeeth no.846 in *Kitāb ul-Adhān, 'Bāb yastaqbal al-Imām an-Nās'* [Chapter: The Imām Faces the People]; Muslim, vol.1, p.83-84, hadeeth no.71 in *Kitāb ul-Adhān, 'Bāb Bayān Kafara man Qāl Matarnā bi'n-Naw'* [Chapter: Explaining the Disbelief of the One Who Says "We Were Rained Upon by the Planets"]. Both hadeeth are from 'Ubaydullāh bin 'Abdullāh from Zayd bin Khālid al-Juhanī in *marfū'* form and it is a *hadeeth qudsī*.

[2] Loving other than Allāh as one should love Allāh is *shirk*, Allāh says, **"And [yet], among the people are those who take other than Allāh as equals [to Him]. They love them as they [should] love Allāh. But those who believe are stronger in love for Allāh."** *{Baqarah (2): 165}* And likewise fearing other than Allāh as Allāh should be feared is *shirk*, Allāh says, **"So do not fear the people but fear Me..."** *{al-Mā'idah (5): 44}* And Allāh says, **"So fear them not, but fear Me, if you are [indeed] believers."** *{Āli 'Imrān (3): 175}* As for natural fear while still believing that benefit and harm is in the Hand of Allāh alone then that is not *shirk* and there is no problem with this, Allāh says about Mūsā ﷺ, **"So he left it, fearful and anticipating [apprehension]."** *{al-Qasas (28): 21}*

[3] It is mentioned in a hadeeth: *"Whoever prays to be seen has committed shirk and whoever gives charity to be seen has committed shirk and whoever fasts to be seen has committed shirk."* Its verification has been mentioned prior. Allāh says in regards to the one who does actions for the *dunya* (the worldly life), **"Whoever desires the life of this world and its adornments – We fully repay them for their deeds therein, and they therein will not be**

15. Obeying the *'Ulama* (scholars) and *Umarā* (rulers) in disobeying Allāh, and prohibiting what Allāh has made *halāl* and legalising what Allāh has made *harām*.[1]

16. Setting up partners with Allāh.[2]

17. Swearing oaths by other than Allāh.[3]

18. Comparing the will of Allāh with the will of the creation by saying for example *"whatever Allāh wills and so-and-so wills."*[4]

19. Cursing time.[5]

---

deprived. Those are the ones for whom there is not in the Hereafter but the Fire. And lost is what they did therein, and worthless is what they used to do." *{Hūd (11): 15-16}*

[1] Allāh says, **"They have taken their scholars and monks as lords besides Allāh, and [also] the Messiah, the son of Mary. And they were not commanded except to worship one God; there is no deity except Him."** *{at-Tawbah (9): 31}* This is because they made lawful for them what Allāh had made unlawful and deemed as unlawful what Allāh has made lawful for them, and obeyed them in this so that was their worship of their scholars and monks other than worshipping Allāh. In a hadeeth it says: *"Obedience is only in that which is good"*, the hadeeth is agreed upon from the hadeeth of 'Ali ﷺ in *marfū'* form.

[2] Those who set up partners with Allāh in His Judgement, Divine Legislation, command or anything else, making Allāh equal with something else and obeying them.

[3] As in the hadeeth: *"Whoever swears an oath to other than Allāh has disbelieved or committed shirk."* Its verification has been mentioned beforehand.

[4] The Prophet ﷺ said to the one who said that: *"Are you making me a partner with Allāh? Rather say 'whatever Allāh wills and then what you will'."* Its verification has been mentioned beforehand.

[5] In a *hadeeth qudsī* it is stated: *"The son of Adam harms me by cursing time, and time is in my Hand, I bring about the night and day."* The hadeeth is agreed upon from the hadeeth of Abū Hurayrah ﷺ in *marfū'* form.

20. Naming someone as "*the judge of judges*".[1]

21. Making fun of something which mentions Allāh.[2]

22. Seeking intercession with Allāh by one of his creation.[3]

---

[1] This is because the true Judge of judges is Allāh and none can reject his judgement, some '*Ulama* however did allow this term to be applied in a restricted sense like when someone says for example: "*the judge of the judges of Yemen*" or the likes.

[2] Allāh says, **"Say, "Is it Allāh and His verses and His Messenger that you were mocking?" Make no excuse; you have disbelieved after your belief."** {*at-Tawbah (9): 65-66*} Making mockery of something which mentions Allāh is a dangerous matter indeed.

[3] Based on the hadeeth: *"Intercession with Allāh is not to be made via anyone"* reported by Abū Dāwūd and other from the hadeeth of Jubayr bin Mut'am ﷺ within a long story. However the hadeeth is *da'eef*. Refer to the book *Ma La Budda Minhu*, pp.27-29.

⇥ Conclusion ⇤

All praise is due to Allāh who with His Virtue completes righteous actions as He granted success in completing this book in clarifying *shirk* and the means to it according to the *Hanbalī 'Ulama* which completes the series. In respect of what has been mentioned in the introduction regarding our avoidance of referring to Shaykh ul-Islām Ibn Taymiyyah, his student Ibn ul-Qayyim, Shaykh Ibn 'AbdulWahhāb and the Imāms of *da'wah* then this was so that no one would think that they were the only ones (from the *Hanābilah*) who spoke on this issue. Even if we did transmit from them in the subject that would be very lengthy and would sub-divide into sections due to them having authored sole works and huge classifications on the subject. Then *bida'* (religious innovations) became widespread within teaching and authoring, to the extent that the term *"Ahl us-Sunnah wa'l-Jama'ah"* was used by the people of *bida'* and the deviant schools of thought who had heretical creeds, rather indeed, you will see them monopolising the term for themselves. As for the *Hanābilah* and the Ahl ul-Hadeeth then they were nicknamed as *"Taymiyūn"*[1] and *"Wahhābis"*[1] and were accused of

---

[1] They abusively nicknamed as being "Taymiyyūn", refer to: Ibn Marzooq, *Barā't ul-Ash'areen*, pp.169, 186, 187, 189; and also Ibn Marzūq, *at-Tawassul bi'n-Nabī*, pp.100, 113, 114, 116.

revolting, anthropomorphism *(tajseem)* and being worthless ones *(Hashwiyyah)*.

To the extent that many of the common people apply these terms (i.e. "*Wahhābi*") to Ahl us-Sunnah due to the death of knowledge and practice in accordance with the Book and the Sunnah, also due to the role of kings and leaders helping the people of innovation. The people of innovation then made up a principle to justify what they were doing and this principle divided *bida'* into being "good" *(hasanah)* or "reprehensible" *(sa'iyyah)*. They then made these religious innovations seem good by claiming that they indicated "*love of the Prophets*" and "*love of the righteous*" and sanctioned venerating the Prophets and dead pious (Muslims) and seeking blessings from them. This is the origin of extremism that the people of the scripture fell into, Allāh says,

﴿قُلْ يَا أَهْلَ الْكِتَابِ لاَ تَغْلُواْ فِي دِينِكُمْ غَيْرَ الْحَقِّ وَلاَ تَتَّبِعُواْ أَهْوَاء قَوْمٍ قَدْ ضَلُّواْ مِن قَبْلُ وَأَضَلُّواْ كَثِيرًا وَضَلُّواْ عَن سَوَاء السَّبِيلِ﴾

"Say: O People of the Scripture do not go to excess in your religion without right, and do not follow the desires of a people who went astray before..." *{al-Mā'idah (5): 77}*

Allāh also says,

---

[1] Refer to *al-Ma'yār ul-Mu'arab*, vol.11, p.168.

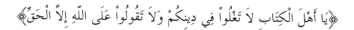

﴿يَا أَهْلَ الْكِتَابِ لاَ تَغْلُواْ فِي دِينِكُمْ وَلاَ تَقُولُواْ عَلَى اللّهِ إِلاَّ الْحَقَّ﴾

**"O People of the Scripture do not go to excess in your religion
and do not say about Allāh except the truth."** *{an-Nisā (4): 171}*

So there is no such thing in Islām as a *"good bida'"* or an *"evil bida'"* as
rather every *bida'* is a misguidance as confirmed from the Prophet ﷺ. As a
result, *bida'* spread and became abundant due to these reasons and also due
to some of the rulers supporting *bida'* to please the ignorant masses and in
response to this favour, some of the blind-following scholars supported
these innovations in order to please the rulers and the common folk. So
then the face of truth became obscured and nearly became wiped out,
innovation became widespread and became the Sunnah. In the meantime
the people of Sunnah became *ghurabā'* (strangers) among the people and
the good became bad while bad became good and the people of innovation
accused the callers to the Sunnah of opposing the majority of people and
for rebelling against the innovations of what the majority were following,
forgetting that the *Jama'ah* is whoever is on the truth even if it is one person
as Ibn Mas'ūd ﷺ stated.

All praise is due to Allāh for preserving this *Ummah* by sending to it one
who will revive the *Deen* and manifest the signs of truth, suppressing
innovation and its people, the people of deviation and misguidance,

refuting the distortions of the extremists, the false pretences of the falsifiers and the interpretations of the ignorant.

With this it is well known that the *'Ulama* of the *Hanābilah* lead the way in this regard and have a major contribution in this field. For this reason some of the ignoramuses label them as being "strict" when the reality is that they call to the Sunnah to be followed and opposing *bida'*, superstitious beliefs and *shirk*. Whether in regards to tombs and graves or making vows, *istighātha*, making *tawāf* around graves and tombs, seeking blessing from graves and tombs, seeking intercession from those in graves and other practices which oppose the guidance of the Prophet ﷺ. They opposed all of this in order to block the avenues to shirk and caution against it and warn from falling into in sayings and actions.

For these reasons I attached utmost importance to this series which has come to an end with the Hanbalī scholars. I ask Allāh to accept this and for good in this intention. Sufficient is Allāh for us and He is the Best disposer of affairs and our final du'ā is all praise is due to Allāh the Lord of the Worlds.

Jamiah Media Publications

Previous Publications:

1. *Before Nicea.* By AbdurRahman Bowes and AbdulHaq al-Ashanti (2005)

2. *Who's in for Iraq?* By Shaykh Abdul'Azeez bin Rayyis ar-Rayyis (2007)

3. *The Impact of Man-Made Laws in the Ruling of an Abode as Being One of Kufr or Islam.* By Shaykh Khalid al-Anbari.(2006)

4. *A Warning Against Extremism.* By Shaykh Salih Aali Shaykh (2008)

5. *A Critical Study of the Multiple Identities and Disguises of 'al-Muhajiroun'.* By Abu Ameenah AbdurRahman as-Salafi and AbdulHaq al-Ashanti (2009).

6. *The Noble Women Scholars of Hadith.* By Shaykh Mashhur Hasan Al Salman. (2010)

7. *The Creed of Imam an-Nawawi,* By Shaykh Mashhur Hasan Al Salman (2010)

8. *The Beautiful Advice to the Noble Salafis of the West,* By Shaykh 'Abdul-Aziz ar-Rayyis (2010)

9. *Shirk According to the 4 Madhhabs.* By Shaykh, Dr Muhammad al-Khumayyis. (2011)

10. *What the Notables Have Narrated About not Going to the Rulers,* Imam Jalalud-Deen as-Suyuti (2011)

11. *'Abdullah el-Faisal al-Jamayki' – A Critical Study of his Statements, Errors and Extremism in Takfir,* By Abu Ameenah AbdurRahman as-Salafi and AbdulHaq al-Ashanti (2011).

Forthcoming Publications:

12. *Guidance on the Ruling on Giving the Khutbah in a Non-Arabic Language.* By Abu Najeed Isam bin Ahmad Saleem bin Mami al-Makki

13. *The Fiqh Madhhab of Ahl ul-Hadith.* By Shaykh Mashhur Hasan Al Salman